How To Pass The Police Recruitment Tests

Visit our How To website at www.howto.co.uk

At www.howto.co.uk you can engage in conversation with our authors –
all of whom have 'been there and done that' in their specialist fields. You
can get access to special offers and additional content but most importantly you will be able to engage with, and become a part of, a wide and
growing community of people just like yourself.

At www.howto.co.uk you'll be able to talk and share tips with people who
have similar interests and are facing similar challenges in their lives. People
who, just like you, have the desire to change their lives for the better – be it
through moving to a new country, starting a new business, growing their
own vegetables, or writing a novel.

At www.howto.co.uk you'll find the support and encouragement you need
to help make your aspirations a reality.

.**How To Books** strives to present authentic, inspiring practical information in their books. Now, when you buy a title from **How To Books,** you
get even more than just words on a page.

How To Pass The Police Recruitment Tests

Kenneth D. Ricketts

Published by How To Books Ltd
Spring Hill House, Spring Hill Road,
Begbroke, Oxford OX5 1RX, United Kingdom
Tel: (01865) 375794. Fax: (01865) 379162
info@howtobooks.co.uk
www.howtobooks.co.uk

How To Books greatly reduce the carbon footprint of their books by
sourcing their typesetting and printing in the UK.

British Library Cataloguing in Publication Data
A catalogue record for this book is available from the British Library

ISBN 978 1 84528 320 9

First edition 2008
Reprinted 2009

Cover design by Mousemat Design Limited
Produced for How to Books by Deer Park Productions, Tavistock
Typeset by Pantek Arts Ltd, Maidstone, Kent
Printed and bound by Cromwell Press Group Ltd, Trowbridge, Wiltshire

NOTE: The material contained in this book is set out in good faith for
general guidance and no liability can be accepted for loss or expense
incurred as a result of relying in particular circumstances on statements
made in this book. Laws and regulations are complex and liable to change,
and readers should check the current position with the relevant authorities
before making personal arrangements.

Contents

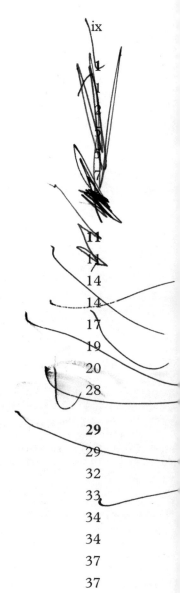

Appendices

Introduction

May I first congratulate you on the purchase of this book and from that purchase, may it take you forward, helping you achieve your goals within this career you have chosen. I will not lie – it holds no simple answers, nor does it hand you the key to the Police Service on a plate. To put it simply, it advises you on what the Service is looking for and points you in the direction of success. Oh, OK then, it does give you a couple of insider tips as well. So where do we start? I guess I'll tell you a little about myself first.

I am 32 years old and have in the past worked as a landscape gardener, sold advertising for a newspaper and held the firm belief that one day I would be a multi-millionaire drummer in a rock band. The band split but the memories and drumsticks remain. I am not a writer (if you hadn't already guessed) but decided to utilise what I have learned about the police recruitment process to aid others, such as yourself, to achieve your goals.

WELL, WHAT DO I KNOW?

I remember my first contact with the Police Service when at junior school. A local bobby would attend our assemblies and give rousing talks on the Service. Something must have stuck because right there and then, I made the choice – 'I want to join the Police.'

There was but one problem to my plan, and a rather huge one at that. I had chosen my career path at the grand age of 8 years, but my local Constabulary at that time, would not take on recruits until they were 21. I knew I had some waiting (and growing) to do but the ambition never left me. It stayed strong throughout my teen years and gave me hope while employed in underpaid, overworked jobs. Then, on my twenty-first birthday, I called the Police Recruitment Department and requested an application form.

I held the application form like a new born baby, for this was the gateway to my dream job. It took some weeks to fill in but after about a month it was in the post, heading back to Police Headquarters with my name all over it. I was overjoyed when I received an invitation to sit my Police exams and even more so when I passed them. By this time, my confidence was at an all-time high. I felt indestructible and was telling friends and family that I was virtually in the door.

Next the physical – easy. I had trained and trained, regularly running two miles every morning as well as an hour on the weights. I breezed through. No one could stop me now. But they did. Along came a mighty dream crusher called 'The Assessment'.

The day was a nightmare from start to finish. It was stress topped with nervous anguish and by the end I felt numb. I had taken part in numerous exercises, both group and individual, performed psychometric tests and role played to the brink. By the end, I was just happy to get out into the fresh air and light a cigarette. A month later my results were posted and my world fell apart – I'd failed.

Now I bet you're thinking – 'Great. I've just spent good money on a book written by an idiot who couldn't get in the Police himself.'

Well, you'd be wrong!

I reapplied after much soul searching in 2000. I passed and soon found myself at the Police clothing stores, fitted out in a brand new uniform. I attended many residential training courses thereafter which I again passed and eventually plodded the beat as a Probationer.

I have now served numerous years in the Police Service and gained many varied skills within that time. Here's a list of what I've achieved to date:

- ***Response Officer*** – attending emergency calls both day and night.
- ***Custody Clerk*** – working in the cell area and dealing with detained individuals.

- ***Van Crew*** – attending the more violent calls and transporting prisoners for others who have performed arrests.

- ***Area Officer/Beat Manager*** – having sole responsibility for a given beat, attempting to reduce priority crime.

- ***Proactive Constable*** – intelligence-led Policing.

During my time I have also done the following:

- studied for and taken my Sergeants exam;

- been interviewed for a position within a Counter Terrorism branch of the Service.

So at least now I hope you have a little more faith in my knowledge and experience!

SO WHY THE BOOK?

When I joined there was little literature out there to help me. The books which were available were all academic and the size of *War and Peace*. I am now well aware that many of you purchase manuals for hundreds of pounds, written by authors who have never actually been out on the streets as an Officer and never taken the tests. Ask yourself the question:

> Who is best to advise me? Somebody who's actually been there, done it and passed or a postgraduate in literature who has researched their subject matter and put together a 1,000-page document with little real thought for the reader?

You work it out!

Since the conception of my idea, I have been overwhelmed by the response of those wishing to help me help others. Not only will I use my own experiences and knowledge to help you, I will use examples and experiences of those that are very new to the job and who have supplied me with relevant, up-to-date material. During the research stage of my book, I have also spoken to those with insider knowledge which I hope will aid you in your quest to pursue your dream.

WHO IS THE BOOK INTENDED FOR?

Well, to put it simply – YOU!

If you've taken the time to purchase the book and read its pages carefully, then you're one step ahead of the rest. It is designed for three specific categories and I'll bet my mortgage you fall into one of them. They are:

1. The *person on the street* who wants to join the Police Service but has not tried to thus far.

2. *Police Community Support Officers* who have tried Police Recruitment but, for whatever reason, have failed to achieve their goals.

3. *Special Constables* who wish to join the regular Service or those that have failed and want to give it another go.

As I've mentioned, I currently serve within one of the UK's many Police Constabularies. Now that may not be the Constabulary you wish to join. Don't panic, you've not wasted your money.

Unlike my day when all the tests were created and run by the Constabulary you wished to join, the recruitment process has become a national entity, run by Centrex. So yes, while some examples I give, for instance within the application stage, will be based on my Constabulary's set forms, all Police Services to a point judge the same criteria. So I can be pretty damn certain that if you follow my advice, you will stand more of a chance of impressing the recruiters from other services around the UK.

SO LET'S GET THE SHOW ON THE ROAD!

Over the next few chapters, I'll explain in detail the recruitment process from start to finish. I'll show you what recruiters are looking for and what they are not. I'll guide you as best I can through each stage giving examples which are clear and simple. This book will not over-complicate matters and will remain simple throughout.

However, please remember I am not you and I cannot anticipate what answers you will give throughout the recruitment process. You and only you know what life experiences you bring to the table. I can only advise you on what is required and what recruiters are looking for. This book is simply a tool which can be used for reference purposes throughout the stages. Pass or fail – it's all in your hands.

Good luck!

Kenneth D. Ricketts

1

What does a Police Officer do?

ALL THAT GLITTERS...

When one of my friends decided he quite fancied joining the Army, he applied through one of the many Armed Forces career centres found jotted about the many towns and cities of the UK. He was taken into a room and shown videos of soldiers skiing on their day off or rock climbing in mountainous regions of Europe, all with tanned, and happy smiling faces.

The truth, as my friend soon found out while enduring basic training for the Army, was vastly different. I guess what I'm trying to point out is that you probably, like me, have no real idea as to what the role of a Police Officer actually is. I certainly went in blind.

As many people do, they watch television and after a series or two of *The Bill*, coupled with *Inspector Morse* and other such fantasies, they feel they know the job inside out. ***You'd be completely wrong*!**

Yes, we do patrol about in our vehicles, investigating crime and arresting criminals but that's only 1% of the job. When I joined some years ago, to say it opened my eyes to the real world is an understatement. The job I do, and the one you are applying for, is like no other I know of. You will see and do many things that 99% of the population could only dream of. So that is why before we even touch on the subject of recruitment, we'd best look at the role in more detail.

WHAT'S IT REALLY ALL ABOUT?

Now I could babble on for pages about the position and explain in vast detail the day-to-day complexities of what is required. *Boring*! Instead I've included a job description for you. If you read its content, and can adapt what is required to the application process, giving **relevant personal** experiences, then you're on the right track to success. The document is on this and the following two pages – I'll explain a little about it later.

> **TIP**
>
> Read through the main duties and responsibilities and try to adapt the bullet points to your everyday life. Some obviously will not be relevant but others will.

JOB DESCRIPTION

Post title: Patrol Constable

Responsible to: Patrol Sergeant

Aim of job: To protect life and property, to maintain order, to prevent and detect crime and to prosecute offenders against the peace

MAIN DUTIES AND RESPONSIBILITIES

Administration

- Maintain records of daily incidents in pocket book where required for evidential purposes.

■ Write reports on incidents attended in accordance with policy or as instructed.

■ Compile initial information and basic files for Crown Prosecution files.

■ Submit crime reports, accident reports, sudden death reports, etc.

■ Prepare summons applications.

■ Complete and submit forms, as required.

■ Be responsible for improving your performance by participating in the Performance Appraisal process with your manager.

Dealing with people

■ Deal with the public in a variety of situations.

■ Liaise and consult with other departments within the Service, e.g. CID, Drug Squad, etc.

■ Liaise and consult with outside agencies such as Social Services, doctors, schools, etc.

■ Liaise with supervisors to set objectives and monitor performance.

■ Promote and comply with policies on equal opportunities and health and safety both in the delivery of services and treatment of others.

Operational duties

- Patrol the beat on foot or by car to maintain law and order, prevent crime, etc.

- Attend court to give evidence.

- Attend scenes of incidents and investigate, such as road traffic collisions, scenes of crime, domestic or other disputes, suspicious circumstances, etc.

- Investigate and detect crime.

- Arrest/summons offenders.

- Gather intelligence on local criminals, possible victims, etc. and liaise with other Officers to update them.

- Execute warrants and serve summonses.

- Take fingerprints/photographs, etc. as required.

- Comply with the National Crime Recording Standard and minimum investigative requirements.

- Ensure compliance with statutory requirements in relation to information management including the Data Protection Act 1998, the Freedom of Information Act 2000 and the Code of Practice on Management of Police Information 2005, as appropriate.

Other resources

- Maintain personal equipment.

So now you know it's a little bit more complicated than television leads you to believe!

WHAT RECRUITERS ARE LOOKING FOR

When you apply to join the Police Service there is a strict marking standard in place. You have to demonstrate specific abilities and experiences within each stage to move you on to the next. Recruiters are not looking for ready-made Officers, but they are looking for potential. That potential will later be trained to comply with the job description given.

Take a good look at the job description again. Can you relate any experiences in your day-to-day life to the *main duties and responsibilities*? If you can, use the pages which follow to scribble down your ideas. These will help you complete the *application stage* later.

Let's start with Administration.

ADMINISTRATION

As a Police Officer, I am sometimes overwhelmed with paperwork, most of which has deadlines or time limits attached. These cannot be overlooked or taken lightly as prosecutions sometimes succeed or fail on my replies to the Crown Prosecution Service. Therefore I am required either to write or type replies in a legible manner, with correct punctuation.

Now obviously we have all been to school and received an education of some sort, but as with me, when you leave and seek work, the need for a pen and the written language is sometimes not needed. As a landscape gardener, I did no writing at all and it is so easy to get out of the habit.

The Police Service expects a certain standard and your initial application form will be the first contact they have with you. Make an impression. (I will talk more about the application stage a little later on.)

EXAMPLE

As an Advertising Sales Representative for a local newspaper, I had sole responsibility for creating revenue through advertising. Within my day-to-day working life, I became adept at working with such applications as Microsoft Excel, Word and other IT-based products to monitor, track and seek new customers.

My duties also included arranging meetings with interested companies who wished to advertise and recording in detail specifics of what they needed the advert to look like. A detailed written report was then submitted to the Editor by me for consideration.

Well, that's my example. Now it's your turn!

Remember to keep this example as you may be able to incorporate it into your application form later on!

DEALING WITH PEOPLE

The Police Service is just that: a service to the public. It relies on communication. As an Officer you will speak to a wide variety of people, from those who want to pass on thanks, to those not so welcoming and who are strictly anti-Police. It also promotes liaison between outside agencies, i.e. housing associations, Social Services, councils and so on.

Now imagine your own experiences with regard to this subject matter. Unless you live on a private island or on top of a mountain, you are bound to have come into contact with many different people. Use these experiences to your advantage.

EXAMPLE

As a landscape gardener, I was routinely given responsibility to manage and take control of the day-to-day running of the business. This allowed me to use initiative and to promote our work to both new customers and those I regularly visited, which in turn led to new contacts being formed via word-of-mouth advertising.

I also formed close associations with new suppliers of material to improve existing relationships. This in turn led to a better service to our clients and the efficient running of the business.

You get the idea. Your turn again!

[blank lined answer box]

OPERATIONAL DUTIES

Now I know that unless you are a serving PCSO (Police Community Support Officer) or Special Constable (volunteer) then there's little on the list in the job description you have done. ***Don't worry***. The Police recruit members of the public, not ready-made Police Officers.

If, however, you have had some sort of experience in the roles mentioned above then this is the time to use it. There is absolutely nothing wrong with blowing your own trumpet.

EXAMPLE

Before my second application to the Police Service, I joined the Special Constabulary to gain experience as a volunteer Officer. Within my time, I took part in investigations into firearms offences, learning such techniques as how to send items for forensic analysis and writing witness statements to the required standard.

During my tours of duty, I also arrested offenders for such matters as shoplifting and public order offences, following strict procedure while in the custody office that adhered to the Codes of Practice for Police Officers. I gained such skills as fingerprinting, the taking of photographs and DNA profiling.

If you can't think of anything to put here, don't worry. If you can, write it down.

> **TIP**
>
> Keep these examples. You can use them later on in your application stage.

So if you can read through the job description and apply your *personal experiences* to what the Service requires, then so far so good.

2

Behavioural competencies

WHAT ARE YOUR EXPECTATIONS OF PEOPLE?

I'd like to start this chapter with a scenario. Read through my example and then fill in what I ask below.

EXAMPLE

You are sitting comfortably in your house reading this book, distracted every now and again by the torrential rain and thunderstorm outside. Suddenly you hear a dripping noise from the other room and when you investigate this, you realise that your roof is steadily letting in water onto your carpet.

Having no experience at roofing yourself, and not knowing anybody else who could help, you reach for the big yellow book and after making contact with a specialist, arrange an appointment so that they can give you a quote and hopefully repair the damaged roof.

Now I'd like you to write seven positive things of what you expect from a good roofer and then seven aspects which you think would be negative.

Positive

1. _____

2. _____

3. _____

4. _____

5. _____

6. _____

7. _____

Negative

1. _____

2. _____

3. _____

4. _____

5. _____

6. _____

7. _____

This scenario actually happened to me and I was given a quote by two separate individuals.

The first arrived in what I can only describe as a large piece of rust on wheels. His van did not display any trade name and his young apprentice couldn't even be bothered to get out and inspect the job at hand.

The roofer himself seemed like a nice chap but spoke to me as if I had been in the trade for years, and tried baffling me with technical terms until I just found myself nodding in agreement most of the time. He inspected my roof from the ground and automatically assumed he knew the fault.

His quote was written on a piece of old card and I was told that I needed to get the job done super fast because he was a very busy man and might not be able to fit me in if I waited. I didn't bother calling him back as you can imagine even though the quote was very reasonable.

The second roofer turned up in his van and it's always reassuring when a company has the confidence to advertise their name and contact details on the side. He asked me to view the roof with him, but I do have an aversion to heights and tend to turn a strange greenish colour at the thought of climbing ladders, so instead he took out his mobile telephone and, using the camera, took pictures of the trouble spots for me. He explained clearly and concisely what the problem was and quoted me on headed paper which again bore his name and contact details. The price was about £200 dearer than the first, but he gave me the confidence in his abilities to hire him for the job. I have had no trouble with the roof since.

I guess the point I'm trying to make here is we all have expectations of people, and their actions and how they behave towards us either strengthens or weakens those expectations.

Police Officers are public servants.

INTRODUCING THE SEVEN BEHAVIOURAL COMPETENCIES

If you fulfil your ambition of becoming a Police Officer, then you will be in constant contact with a wide and varied spectrum of society which expects a standard of service and behaviour appropriate to their needs. As we expect certain standards from a roofer, our expectations are the same with the Police, hence the creation of the seven *behavioural competencies*.

So what are these seven behavioural competencies relating to a Police Officer? They are:

1. Community and customer focus

2. Effective communication

3. Personal responsibility

4. Problem solving

5. Resilience

6. Respect for diversity

7. Team working.

These seven factors will be an important part of your initial application stage and will remain equally important throughout your whole Police career. You must demonstrate each, either orally (during your Assessment day for example) or in written form (your application form). I have spoken to many people who have failed recruitment because they failed to focus on, or did not know and understand, how important the list above actually is.

LOOKING AT THE COMPETENCIES IN PRACTICE

Does this all sound a bit complicated? Don't worry, it's not.

Let's look at it in practical terms. Each of the seven points can be marked either positively or negatively as we did with the roofer earlier. I want to give you another example and I want you to picture yourself as the Police Officer in the scenario.

EXAMPLE

Its 3:30 in the morning and you have been driving alone for some six hours. Suddenly, you receive a report that two terraced houses have been broken into and the offenders are still at the scene. It has also been reported that a vehicle is parked outside one of the two addresses with a male occupant on board.

You are several miles away from the incident, en route back to the station for a well earned cup of coffee and a sandwich because you haven't eaten all day. You recognise one of the addresses being burgled as belonging to a well-known shoplifter. What do you do?

Now I'm not expecting you to know Police procedure or protocol but as the rational, forward thinking individual that I know you are, I want you to answer the following questions as honestly as you can.

Q. Due to the fact you are hungry, tired and one of the victims is a well-known criminal, would you attend this job and why?

Q. Would you treat the family of the shoplifter any different to the respectable family also burgled?

Q. What actions would you put in place en route to stand the best possible chance of capturing the offenders?

Q. A crucial witness does not speak English but may hold vital information. What do you do?

Q. It's now three hours after your shift should have finished. You have found a cigarette butt near to the scene and none of the victims smokes. If you seize it for DNA testing, you may well find yourself at work for another three hours. Would you ignore it?

WHAT DO YOUR RESPONSES DEMONSTRATE?

Now I hope you've been honest with yourself because all Police Officers find themselves in these types of incidents, and even though we all receive the same training, we all act differently. We are all individuals after all.

Let's look at how I would have answered in some detail.

> **Q.** Due to the fact you are hungry, tired and one of the victims is a well known criminal, would you attend this job and why?
>
> I have been to many incidents where the victim of crime has been a well-known criminal element and spent many hours rushing from job to job on an empty stomach but I go. Why? Because that is my duty!

If you have answered like me then you can tick off a positive mark in the competencies of Community and customer focus, Personal responsibility and Resilience.

> **Q.** Would you treat the family of the shoplifter any different to the respectable family also burgled?
>
> Simple answer, no! It's hard in today's society to remain impartial or unbiased but that's exactly what recruiters are looking for. I know they don't want emotionless, robotic zombies either but your personal feelings play no part in the role for which you are applying.

Again if your answer is similar to mine, then tick off Respect for diversity, Resilience and Community and customer focus.

> **Q.** What actions would you put in place en route to stand the best possible chance of capturing the offenders?
>
> I'd make sure the Constabularies surrounding where the crime is being committed are aware of the incident should the suspect vehicle drive off. If available, I'd utilise colleagues to attend the area from different roads so as to stand the best chance of capturing those responsible if they made off either on foot or by car. I'd request a Dog Officer so as to identify any scent tracks left by the perpetrators. The list goes on.

My answer shows Effective communication, Personal responsibility, Problem solving and Team working. How did you do?

> **Q.** A crucial witness does not speak English but may hold vital information. What do you do?
>
> Well you can't very well ignore what they have to say. I'd make contact with an interpreter or seek a member of that person's family to help with the language barrier. Do not allow problems to hinder you or your performance. Remember that, as a Police Officer, nine times out of ten you have been called because a problem needs your attention.

Again, if you can relate your answer to mine, then that's Community and customer focus, Effective communication, Personal responsibility, Problem solving, Resilience and Respect for diversity. Almost a full house!

Q. It's now three hours after your shift should have finished. You have found a cigarette butt near the scene of the crime and none of the victims smokes. If you seize it for DNA testing, you may well find yourself at work for another three hours. Would you ignore it?

I'm afraid not. As much as we want to go home, relax and watch our favourite soap opera, leaving such evidence could have two almighty consequences.

The first is that you are in neglect of your duty for which you will be disciplined. That could be anything from fined, cautioned or sacked.

The second is that this may be the evidence which could identify the offender, so if you don't do your duty and no prosecution is ever brought against that person, you are allowing them to continue in their ways to possibly committing further crime(s).

This answer simply demonstrates Personal responsibility and Resilience.

Now before we go any further, I want you to go back to Chapter 1 and read through your own examples on the subjects of Administration, Dealing with people and Operational duties. Try to see within your answers any of the seven points from the behavioural competencies. I'll be waiting for you below.

LOOKING FOR EVIDENCE OF THE COMPETENCIES

I hope in your examples you can clearly see evidence of the behavioural competencies, either positive or not so. Do not be alarmed if some seem negative – it's a simple task to rewrite your example using some of the knowledge you have now gained to expand your answers and shine for those recruiters.

Let's take one of my examples from Chapter 1.

> As an Advertising Sales Representative for a local newspaper, I had sole responsibility for creating revenue through advertising. Within my day-to-day working life, I became adept at working with such applications as Microsoft Excel, Word and other IT-based products to monitor, track and seek new customers.
>
> My duties also included arranging meetings with interested companies who wished to advertise and recording in detail specifics of what they needed the advert to look like. A detailed written report was then submitted to the Editor by me for consideration.

Seeking new customers, as I have written at the end of the first paragraph, and arranging meetings, mentioned in the second, demonstrate the competencies of Customer focus, Effective communication and Personal responsibility.

Of course, this is just an example and to get it just right I'd expand my answer to demonstrate how, in a positive manner, I performed these tasks and what resulted after my performance.

READY NOW TO FILL IN THAT APPLICATION?

Well, that's exactly what we are going to do in the next chapter. Before we do, though, take the time to read the following pages, which I'll list for you the main positive and negative factors of each competency, so you can refer back to the list as we complete your application form and beyond.

COMMUNITY AND CUSTOMER FOCUS

Positive competence

■ Presents the appropriate image to the public and other organisations.

■ Focuses on the customer in all activities.

■ Sorts out the customer's problems quickly.

■ Apologises when at fault.

■ Responds quickly to customers' requests.

■ Keeps customers updated on progress.

■ Takes pride in delivering high-quality service.

Negative indicators

■ Does not consider individual needs.

■ Does not inform customers as to what is happening.

■ Presents an unprofessional image.

■ Only sees a situation from their own point of view and does not encompass the customer's view.

■ Is slow to respond to customers' requests.

■ Does not check that the needs of the customer are being met.

■ Does not maximise opportunities to talk to people within the community.

EFFECTIVE COMMUNICATION

Positive competence

- Makes sure all written and spoken communication is concise and well structured.

- Communicates in a friendly and approachable style.

- Uses appropriate language and does not use jargon.

- Pays attention to, and shows interest in, what others are saying.

- Listens carefully and understands.

- Asks questions to clarify matters.

- Communicates factual, accurate information and provides it at the right time.

Negative indicators

- Is hesitant, nervous and uncertain when speaking.

- Uses inappropriate language or jargon.

- Does not consider the target audience.

- Writes in an unstructured way.

- Does not listen and constantly interrupts others.

- Assumes others have understood without actually checking that they have.

- Avoids answering difficult questions.

PERSONAL RESPONSIBILITY

Positive competence

- Accepts personal responsibility for decisions and actions.

- Displays initiative, taking on tasks without being asked.

- Keeps promises and does not let colleagues down.

- Takes pride in their own work.

- Follows things through to a satisfactory conclusion.

- Is self-motivated and displays dedication to their role.

- Is aware of their own strengths and weaknesses.

Negative indicators

- Is not concerned about letting others down.

- Will not deal with issues, hoping they will just go away.

- Blames others rather than admitting to mistakes.

- Puts in the least effort in order to just get by.

- Gives up easily when faced with problems.

- Fails to recognise personal weaknesses and development needs.

- Displays a negative or disruptive attitude.

PROBLEM SOLVING

Positive competence

- Identifies where to get information and gets it.

- Takes in all information quickly and accurately.

- Identifies what can and cannot be changed.

- Remains impartial and avoids jumping to conclusions.

- Makes good decisions that take into account all the factors.

- Gets as much appropriate information as possible.

- Takes a systematic approach to solving problems.

Negative indicators

- Does not gather sufficient information before jumping to conclusions.

- Does not consult other people who may have extra information.

- Does not gather evidence.

- Becomes distracted by minor issues.

- Reacts without considering all angles.

- Does not notice or deal with a problem until it has become something more significant.

- Makes assumptions about the facts.

RESILIENCE

Positive competence

- Deals confidently with members of the public, drawing on their own skills and abilities.

- Is comfortable working alone with an appropriate level of supervision.

- Is aware of and manages their own stress.

- Accepts criticism and praise.

- Says 'no' when necessary.

- Takes a rational and consistent approach to work.

- Shows patience when dealing with people who complain.

Negative indicators

- Gets easily upset, frustrated and annoyed.

- Walks away from confrontation when it would be more appropriate to get involved.

- Needs constant reassurance, support and supervision.

- Uses inappropriate physical force.

- Complains about problems rather than dealing with them.

- Worries about making mistakes so avoids difficult situations wherever possible.

- Deals with situations aggressively.

RESPECT FOR DIVERSITY

Positive competence

- Sees issues from other people's viewpoints.

- Is polite, tolerant and patient with people, treating them with respect and dignity.

- Shows understanding and is sensitive to people's problems and vulnerabilities.

- Uses language in an appropriate way and is sensitive to the way it may affect people.

- Acknowledges and respects a broad range of social and cultural customs, beliefs and values within the law.

- Challenges inappropriate attitudes, language and behaviour that is abusive, aggressive or discriminatory.

- Takes into account the personal needs and interests of others.

Negative indicators

- Does not consider other people's feelings.

- Makes situations worse by using inappropriate remarks, language or behaviour.

- Does not respect confidentiality.

- Shows bias and prejudice when dealing with people.

- Is dismissive of and impatient with people.

- Does not encourage people to talk about personal issues.

- Criticises people without considering their feelings and motivation.

TEAM WORKING

Positive competence

- Understands their own role within a team.

- Actively supports and assists the team in reaching objectives.

- Makes time to get to know people.

- Offers to help others.

- Accepts help from others when needed.

- Develops mutual trust and confidence in others.

- Willingly takes on unpopular or routine tasks.

Negative indicators

- Does not volunteer to help other members of the team.

- Takes credit for success without recognising the contribution(s) of others.

- Has their own agenda.

- Plays one person off against another.

- Does not let people say what they think.

- Does not offer advice when others seek it.

- Shows little interest in working jointly with other groups.

STOP, TAKE A BREATH AND EVALUATE

So, we've come to the end of the first two chapters and by now I'm quite sure some of your heads are starting to hurt. I told you this was like nothing you've ever seen on television.

In the next chapter, I will take you step by step through the initial application form – that's if I've not already put you off the job. Before we do, I just want to reiterate the two points I've tried to achieve in these first two chapters. They are:

1. The role for which you are applying is wide and varied and the training and knowledge you receive never ends throughout.

2. Use the information I have supplied to provide evidence for yourself in your application form. Try as best you can to fit in examples of your everyday life which relate in whatever way to the role of a Police Officer and the behavioural competencies we adhere to.

Do the latter and you're one step closer to becoming a PC.

3

The application form

I was that scared of filling the damn thing in, I got my mum to do it. (Quote from a recent applicant)

IT'S ALL A SIMPLE MATTER OF R.T.F.Q.

When I first applied for the Police Service, there was never any time limit imposed for completing and sending the application form back. Good job really! It took my sorry behind about a month before I read it and another two before I plucked up the nerve to fill the damn thing out.

These days, however, some Constabularies register your name at the recruitment office when you request your application pack and quote a time limit in which they want it back, fully completed. If you fail to do as requested, you're going no further on this journey and all your blood, sweat and tears will have gone to waste.

This added pressure forces some of us to rush and that's when mistakes start to happen. That is why we will start with a phrase commonly used in most Police Services today: **R.T.F.Q.**

Before I let the cat out of the bag and explain what this stands for, I've a little test for you. I'm simply trying to prove a point.

All I want you to do is read out loud exactly what you see on the next page. If you can, ask a friend or family member to do the same. I guarantee they will repeat what you read.

RIP

Here lies the

the body of

Sally M Charles

8.2.49 – 2.1.07

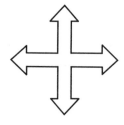

I'm not usually a betting man … but I guarantee 90% of you will have read it completely wrong. I bet you've read:

RIP, Here lies the body of Sally M Charles.

My point, other than feeling a little smug, is that when you are faced with something that is alien to you, for example the Police application form or the illustration you've just read, you rush certain aspects and miss salient points. Your eyes register only part of what is being asked/stated and your brain fills in the rest. I know this because what you should have read is –

RIP, Here lies the the body of Sally M Charles.

Easy to miss, I know. So, now to the phrase we started with:

R.T.F.Q. = Read The F***ing Question

I am sorry for putting it bluntly, but that was the exact phrase used to get me through my initial training exams, followed by my Sergeants exam and other similar exam-type scenarios.

So many people fail at the application stage, not because of lack of life experience or failing to cross a 't' and missing the odd full stop. Simply put, they fail to read the question in its entirety which culminates in the recruiters reading paragraph after paragraph of waffle.

If you get this wrong, you'll have to wait between *six* and *twelve* months before you can re-apply. Do not fail at the very first hurdle.

Before we begin on the application itself, please read my helpful list of dos and don'ts. Refer back to them if necessary as you complete the application pack.

Dos

1. *Treat the application form with care.* No dog-eared corners, coffee marks, etc.

2. Make a *photocopy* of the application (all parts) and complete this in pencil (not pen, as you can't rub out mistakes).

3. R.T.F.Q – read the question at least twice before attempting to answer.

4. Complete all sections *fully*. Do not miss out any section. Those that don't apply, simply mark as N/A (not applicable).

5. *Use correct punctuation, capital letters, commas and full stops. Write in paragraphs.*

6. Get a *second opinion* about your answers. You may have missed something that somebody else notices.

7. When the time comes to fill in the real forms, *take your time*.

8. Use *black* ball point pen where indicated to do so.

9. If you make a mistake, don't worry. Simply place *one single diagonal line* through your mistake. Do not attempt to overwrite.

10. *Personalise your answers.* The recruitment team doesn't want to know how your team did; they want to know about you.

I've highlighted the key words for you. I know it sounds like child's play and really, really simple, but I know of colleagues who failed to get it right first time around, as I did, and had a lengthy wait before trying again.

DON'TS

1. *Rush* to get the thing completed. Give yourself time.

2. *Write anything which may offend*. (Remember the behavioural competencies.)

3. *Forget to include any section of the form when returning it*.

4. Forget to make sure you've *paid the required postage* and packaging. If you don't, you will never receive any notification because the Royal Mail simply won't deliver it.

5. *Lie*. The truth will always out. Be yourself.

6. *Generalise* your answers. Give specifics.

Again, I know the list sounds a little like a nursery lesson, but I really wouldn't write them down if the points made were not of vast importance and imperative to get right.

I'd like to bring your attention to *point 3* on the 'Don'ts' list.

Your application pack will contain different forms which I will discuss on the following pages. Some of the forms, for example the equal opportunities questionnaire, seem less important, say, than the application booklet. If you fail to send any section back to the recruiters, ask yourself one question:

Are the recruiters going to spend time chasing you up?

COMPLETING THE FORMS

Unlike the nationalised assessment day which a successful candidate will progress to after the application stage, each Constabulary has their own application pack containing forms unique to them. For example, recently I requested two application packs from adjoining Constabularies and they were completely different. Even so, the questions asked were seeking the same criteria.

Therefore it would be a pointless exercise to fill the next hundred pages with every question from every force in the UK. I'm here to help you to answer those questions, maximising your potential in the process. I want you to know how to answer *any* question they ask, not just a specific one.

THE REGISTRATION FORM

This form may be pink in colour with numerous small boxes throughout (though this may vary from force to force).

- Complete all sections *on **both sides*** of the form.

- Use *pencil*, not pen.

- *Sign* and *date* where requested (usually at the very bottom of the underside).

- *Take your time* – there is no rush.

This form is of huge importance as it supplies whatever Constabulary you are applying for with all your personal details. It is designed to be read by computer, hence the strange layout. Check and double check you have completed all sections and there are no mistakes. ***DO NOT BEND THIS DOCUMENT***.

It may seem a little complicated to fill out at first so I'll show you a quick example of how to do it. The next two examples will be similar to the section of the form asking for your name.

EXAMPLE

A B C D E F G H I J K L M N O P Q R S T U V W X Y

1 []

2 []

3 []

4 []

5 []

6 []

7 []

8 []

9 []

This example shows the form before completion. Let's now assume it asks for my name. What do you do? I'll show you.

	A	B	C	D	E	F	G	H	I	J	K	L	M	N	O	P	Q	R	S	T	U	V	W	X	Y
1											~														
2				~																					
3														~											
4														~											
5			~																						
6																				~					
7							~																		
8																									
9																									

I've taken away the boxes to try and make it a little clearer. My name, Kenneth, has now been inputted onto the form in the proper manner. As you can see, for each letter in my name, I have moved down a line. So the letter K corresponds with the number 1, the letter E corresponds with the number 2 and so on and so forth.

Remember, this is a computer-read form so if you make any mistake, no matter how small or insignificant, you could jeopardise your application.

THE APPLICATION FORM

This form takes the shape of a small booklet. Again, between forces, they will vary somewhat but *all* application forms take a similar format.

Before you go any further with this section of the form, take it to your local library or current place of work, photocopy it and then place it safely to one side. Practise in pencil on the copied form and have a dictionary to hand. This booklet is where you can either shine or fall by the wayside. Treat it with care.

I once bought a computer and was so excited about getting it set up I ignored the instructions and set it up myself. To this day I have no clue what I did wrong but the loud BANG and subsequent smell of smoke from the plug socket told me I had messed up. It cost me nearly £100 to get the problem fixed.

My point – there will be a section, either separate or within the booklet, guiding you on how to fill in the application correctly. Take time to read it at least twice. Do not ignore it or simply discard it. It is included for a reason – *to help you*.

Now I do not know each of you individually and cannot answer the questions for you. I can only guide you, so let's make a start.

SECTION 1 – ABOUT YOU

Quite self-explanatory really! Simply input your personal details into the boxes provided.

■ Use black pen and make sure your writing is neat and legible.

■ Do not leave any box unanswered.

This section, as with the registration document, simply introduces you to the recruiters. The boxes will include such questions as your name, date of birth, current address and telephone number.

So far, so good ...

SECTION 2 – ABOUT YOUR EMPLOYMENT

Again, I cannot really say anything about your previous work history. Just fill out **all** the boxes provided.

- Continue to use *black pen throughout*. Keep the form *neat* and *tidy*.

- Give **specific** dates regarding your employment history.

- Any boxes that do not apply to you **do not** leave blank. Mark as **N/A**.

- *Do not lie* about your references. Unlike some jobs you may have applied for in the past, the Police Service *does* check.

Have you ever completed a CV for employment purposes? If so, there's little I can advise you about this section. If not, I'll explain how to set your examples out.

Most applications will ask for, or look like, the following example:

Date of employment	Job title	Brief description of duties	Reason for leaving

It is important to understand that, when completing this section, you must always start with your most recent employer and work backwards. Let's say, for example, I wanted to apply for a job that required my CV. It would look something like this:

Date of employment	Job title	Brief description of duties	Reason for leaving
2000 – Present	Police Officer	Maintain law and order	Pursue new career aspects
1997 – 2000	Landscaper	Block paving Patio laying	To join the police
1995 – 1997	Sales Rep	Selling advertising	Redundancy

I know my example is short but I hope you get the idea.

SECTION 3 – ABOUT YOUR EDUCATION SKILLS

Again this part falls to you. Just remember the following:

■ When listing the schools, colleges or universities you have attended, *always* put the most recent first.

■ *List* your qualifications. *Do not* write entire sentences about what you achieved at school.

This part should be completed exactly the same as the section asking for your employment history. The two go hand in hand.

SECTION 4 – COMPETENCY ASSESSMENT

Right! So now comes the tricky bit! You've completed the first part of your application and all is good. You've turned the page and seen what now lies ahead – fact-based questions that could decide your future!

Before you fill them in, I want to give you *three* tips that will impress the socks off the recruitment team. *Use these tips to complete all the following questions*.

R.T.F.Q.

As we mentioned earlier, take your time and read each part of the question. Make sure you have it set in stone in your head. By now you should have to hand Chapters 1 and 2 of this book regarding the role of an Officer and the behavioural competencies, the list of 'Dos' and 'Don'ts' contained within this chapter and the photocopy of the booklet on which to write.

S.T.A.R.

Let's say for example I decide to become a Firearms Officer when a vacancy arises. Just like you are doing now, I too have to fill in an application form for an internal Police post. This application then gets forwarded, first to the Police recruitment team who assess the examples I have given and then on to managers of the department for which I am applying.

My application form gets marked in exactly the same way as yours will. It is a usual occurrence that for every one post open, twenty Officers will apply, so the competition is hot. I have since learned the marking method which recruiters use and, if you follow it correctly, hopefully your responses will grab their attention and place you at the top of their list. That method is known as S.T.A.R.

Situation
Task
Actions
Result

So what I want you to do now is look at any of the questions you are now facing and on a scrap piece of paper write down your answer using the S.T.A.R. principle.

EXAMPLE

Q. Explain a time in your life when you have faced confrontation.

First, we must explain the **situation**:

In November of last year, while I was out with friends in a local public house, a male approached and began to argue with one of my friends. His manner was aggressive and I could see he was spoiling for a fight. My friend, not knowing what to do, turned to me for advice.

Secondly, we must explain what **task** was now set because of the situation:

I could see that my friend feared for his personal safety as the male continued with a verbal barrage. Due to my current position within the Police Service and the fact that families with small children were eating nearby, I attempted to calm the male and resolve his issue.

Thirdly, what **actions** were put in place because of the task?

I stood up from my table, approaching the male in a calm, sociable way, stepping between him and my friend. I spoke softly and clearly asking what the problem was and what could be done to resolve the matter.

And finally, what was the **result** of those actions?

> The male calmed down and stepped away from the area in which my friend sat. He spoke of his problem and then left, apologising to me for his behaviour.

And that is how you must now answer the competency assessment questions. Structure each individual question to clearly show the S.T.A.R. principle. Don't forget, if you can, to add in those all-important behavioural competencies. The more detail you get in, the more impressed the recruiters will be.

Personalise

I want you to read the following two statements.

STATEMENT 1

I play for a local football team and we recently won the challenge cup. We had to play six matches in total and won every one. We are now top of the league.

STATEMENT 2

I play left back for my local football team. I have contributed through training and matches fully and, as part of the team, helped to win the challenge cup.

I know it sounds simple but you'd be surprised how many people make the mistake illustrated here. Statement 1 talks more about the football team. However, the recruiters are not hoping to employ a team or business, they want to know about the applicant – YOU! So Statement 2 focuses on you and the contribution you made to the team's success. It is more personal.

There is absolutely nothing wrong with blowing your own trumpet on the application form. Every answer you give must be relevant to the question asked and, more importantly, demonstrate *your* abilities.

I recently spoke to a Sergeant who interviews applicants at the final stage of recruitment. His exact words were:

> The reason why most people fail is they don't **personalise** their answers. There's too much, well we did this and we did that, and not enough about what **I** did.

So I hope now the prospect of answering those all-important questions is a little less daunting.

As I've mentioned, I do not know which Constabulary you may be applying for so can't know the questions with which you are faced. I hope though I've given you all the tools and knowledge available to make the task a little easier and pushed you enough towards being one of the successful candidates asked back to attend the Assessment day.

DON'T FORGET ...

Usually towards the back of the application form there will be other pages to be completed. They usually comprise an equal opportunities questionnaire, a marketing form, a declaration and a check list. *Fill them all in.*

Once you are satisfied that all is complete, *check*, *check* and *check* again. If you fail to send something you should have, you fail regardless, so it's worth the extra fuss.

And remember, if you need any other advice about the application form or its completion, simply phone up the recruitment office. All the numbers are provided for you in Appendix 1 at the back of the book.

4

The assessment centre – introduction

TAKING CARE OF THE PRELIMINARIES

Congratulations if you've passed the paper sift for the application stage (and you really should have if you've read this book) and have been invited by your prospective Constabulary to take part in the assessment day.

Before we go any further take note of the following advice:

1. **Eat well** before attending. It's a long day and a hearty breakfast will give you the required energy.

2. **Dress appropriately.** You are applying for a profession which prides itself on image. Males – wear a suit and tie with your shoes polished. Females – smart dress or suit.

3. **Read the information provided** by your Constabulary prior to attending. Bring all the required information they request. As with my Constabulary, they first require the following:

   ■ Contact recruitment to confirm your attendance for the day.

   ■ Bring with you the assessment invitation letter.

   ■ Forms of identification with you to allow registration, e.g.

     – full 10-year passport *or two* of the following:

     – British driving licence;

- P45;

- birth certificate – issued within six weeks of birth;

- cheque book or bank card – with three statements and proof of signature

- proof of residence - such as a council tax, gas or electricity bill.

If you fail to bring any of this documentation, then you're going home.

4. *Be punctual*. Always allow enough time for your journey. Remember the day will start early in the morning so give time for rush-hour traffic, etc. Always arrive *15 minutes* prior to the time given. If you're late, YOU'VE FAILED.

Don't be the one candidate who walks away before the day begins.

WHAT EXACTLY IS AN ASSESSMENT DAY?

At this moment in time, you've impressed the recruiters enough with the content of your application form. They have probably sifted through hundreds of potential candidates and selected the few who achieved the required mark. Of course, at this stage, although they like what they have read, they do not know you or even know what you look like.

Let's put it another way. Some people when applying for employment tend to exaggerate skills and abilities and write themselves into a position that they simply are not qualified to do. The assessment centre not only introduces the candidate to their prospective employer, it allows them to observe you in action. To put it simply, it assesses your abilities compared to those necessary for the role applied for.

Unlike when I first applied and took part in the assessment day, today it is a national entity and run by a company called CENTREX. There are two distinct advantages to this:

1. If you do happen to fail first time around (as I did), if you choose to apply for a neighbouring Constabulary, the assessment day remains the same which gives you a head start on other new candidates.

2. If you pass the national assessment day, you can if you so desire contact other UK forces and choose which one you join. This was unheard of when I applied but I know of one person who has done so.

The day itself is long and tiring and by the end your head will ache. You will sit outside with other candidates who have undergone the same stresses as you, and talk yourself out of the position. You will be so sure that others performed so much better and wonder why you even tried.

STOP!

When the day has finished, simply walk away and try as best you can to forget about it. What's done is done and worrying yourself to sleep over the next few nights will not change a thing. If you pass you pass, if you fail you fail.

WHAT DOES THE DAY ENTAIL?

In the following chapters I go through the types of exercises that you will undergo throughout the day. Other literature out there will claim to tell you the precise exercises you will undertake. They are talking rubbish. Recruitment teams throughout the UK regularly change each exercise for two specific reasons:

1. It stops candidates telling others how to pass because they have been there.

2. It simply keeps the assessment centre, its examiners and role players fresh with no chance of them stagnating.

How do I know this? Well, before writing this book I spoke with recruiters in an attempt to procure the specific assessment tests. They told me that the day and the tests are regularly changed because of the reasons given above.

However, although the tests are changed, the general process and marking stay the same. If you prepare beforehand, then you're already halfway to passing the day.

The day is split into five categories. These are:

1. Two written exercises lasting 20 minutes each.

2. Four role-playing/interactive exercises, each lasting ten minutes (five minutes for preparation/five minutes for the actual activity).

3. Numerical reasoning test (12 minutes).

4. Verbal logical reasoning test (25 minutes long).

5. Interview comprising four questions, allowing the candidate five minutes per question (total time 20 minutes).

Now for those of you that are new to Police recruitment I'm pretty sure you've read the list above, had a sharp intake of breath and wondered how on earth you'll make it through the day. So, in the following chapters we'll break each test down in detail.

5

The assessment centre – written exercises

Can you read letters of complaint from two parties and, taking both opinions into account, respond with a letter of suggestion to appease both?

- YES – well that's exactly what the assessors are looking for.

- NO – well I suggest you get practising.

WHAT IS EXPECTED OF YOU

The assessment centre will provide you with documentation from two or three persons, complaining about each other's behaviour, the way they have been treated or within a political agenda, e.g. parking problems within a specific location. The assessors want you simply to read all the information provided and choose the salient points from all concerned. They then expect you to respond to all parties, in the form of a professionally written letter, using correct punctuation and spelling. They also expect you to pick up on matters which involve five core competencies:

1. *Respect for race and diversity*. Read what is in front of you carefully. Pick up and challenge any matters relating to this subject matter. Failure to do so lowers your overall score.

2. *Written communication*. The letter needs to appease all parties while being non-judgemental and unbiased. Write the letter neatly, clearly and with correct punctuation. Set it out professionally.

3. *Effective communication*. The letter can't just ramble on and on with no real reasoning. There has to be an aim, a strong but fair explanation and a conclusion with relevant and pertinent suggestions to the parties involved.

4. *Problem solving*. You are writing this letter with one aim in mind – customer satisfaction! Think reasonably, taking all sides into account. Do not side with one or the other. Formulate a plan of action within the letter which shows clear and concise decision-making.

5. *Team working*. In your letter, give suggestions on how to implement your ideas using members of your team as well as outside agencies. Remember your letter is there to satisfy all involved and show a willingness to help.

TIP

- *Watch your spelling*. Get it right.

- *Use paragraphs and lots of them*. Keep your sentences reasonably short.

- *Do not use abbreviations*, for example e.g., etc., and so on.

- *Outline the background* of all parties to show clear understanding.

- Suggest *pertinent resolutions* to whatever problem you are dealing with.

- *Be unbiased, non-judgemental and non-political*.

- Remember and memorise *the core competencies*.

- Study other official letters sent to you, perhaps from your bank manager or mortgage lender, to see exactly how to set a letter out correctly.

Remember I cannot give you the exact scenarios which you will face on the day but I am able to give you an example of what it may be like:

> **EXAMPLE**
>
> You are the manager of a local health club which comprises a weights room, spa and cardio area. You have held the position for five years and have a team of 15 people around you. Your employees range from the ages of 18 up to 50 years. There are no undue problems within the health club as far as you are aware.

SETTING THE BACKGROUND

So the test has started. You have now been made aware of your current position with a little background behind it. Next you will be faced with two letters. They will usually look something like this:

Mrs A Edwards
3 Edwards Avenue
Manchester
PO BOX 33

Today's date

Area Manager
Local Heath Club
Manchester,
M11 1QQ

For the attention of the Area Manager

I am writing this letter of complaint regarding the actions of a staff member at one of your local health clubs last Saturday. I have thought about not putting pen to paper but need to air my views as I feel strongly about the incident.

I had always thought staff at your premises were polite and well trained but nothing shocked me more when I overheard a conversation involving a male member of your staff insulting another gym user simply because of her weight. Furthermore, the language used was, I believe, not in keeping with the standards you expect.

I would also like to express my concern over the expansion of the weights room. I have been a loyal member of your club for many years but feel your members who simply want to participate in aerobics are being pushed to one side to allow a more spit-and-sawdust gym to take precedence.

I therefore would like to know what actions you will be taking and can only hope for the sake of sanity the young man involved be removed from his current position.

I await your response.

Yours faithfully

Mrs A Edwards

Area Manager
Local Health Club HQ
Manchester
M11 1QQ

Today's date

Local Manager
Local Heath Club
Manchester
M11 1QQ

For the attention of the Local Manager

I have just received correspondence from a member of our health club wishing to complain about the conduct of a staff member last Saturday.

Mrs A Edwards is expressing concern over certain choice language but further explains, quite worryingly for the company, alleged name calling of our members.

You have been the Local Manager at our premises now for some years and I am quite sure you are aware of company policy. Therefore I want this matter resolved with whatever course of action you feel necessary.

Could you also please advise her re the expansion of the weights room?

Please don't hesitate to contact me if you have any further queries.

So there are the two letters, expressing concern and complaints. (Remember, these are simply made up, and are not exact examples from real life.)

WHAT TO DO NEXT

By now you should have read both letters and understood any problems or complaints. My example is quite short as I simply want to show you, first, what the test will look like and, secondly, the importance of picking up all the salient points.

I want you now to go back to the first letter and write down all the points you think should be addressed.

1. _____

2. _____

3. _____

4. _____

5. _____

6. _____

7. _____

8. _____

Now I hope after scribbling them down you can formulate some sort of action plan by which the complaint can be dealt with effectively and quickly.

Take a look at mine:

---

1. The company invites letters from customers expressing concerns as it always takes the views of its customers into account. After all, the company provides a service to its members.

2. Discrimination will not be tolerated. Should the allegation be proved then formal disciplinary proceedings will be instigated. If, for whatever reason, no such behaviour or activity is discovered, the company may suggest training courses for its entire staff to alleviate any further problems.

3. We take all concerns seriously, especially from those customers who feel their training activity is being affected by the expansion of the weights room. At present the expansion is due to continue but the company will release customer questionnaires to every member to gauge further opinion.

Right! Now you've formulated a plan and response to the complainant, complete a single letter constructed like the two examples given, including the points which you feel of importance.

TRY ANOTHER EXAMPLE

Let's try another example.

You are a local councillor and have just been voted by your constituents serve for another term. You have promised in your manifesto swift action against anti-social behaviour and to target congestion which is a prevalent problem within your town centre. You are also targeting littering and have instigated action teams who carry out daily inspections on your behalf.

You have been a member of the committee within the town hall for seven years, but the newly appointed mayor disagrees with your policies, and it is your opinion that he has tried to overrule most of your arguments due to political differences. You are striving to become mayor as your political career progresses.

As before, you are introduced to a little background knowledge before being faced with two opposing letters. Use your allocated time wisely and digest and retain the available information.

Try to picture yourself in the role you are taking on and think and feel how the Councillor would act on a day-to-day basis. Picture their surroundings and allow yourself for a brief time to take on the attributes of that person.

Having done this, read the two letters carefully, picking out all the salient points which you will use later to respond in letter form and thus complete the exercise.

I think I did alright on the Assessment day but messed up on the two written exercises. I even think that I forgot to write in paragraphs and just mumbled on to fill the page. (Quote from a failed candidate)

So let's now read and absorb the two letters that make up this exercise.

Mr A Smith
3 Your Street
Your District
Your Town
Postcode

Today's date

The Local Councillor
Town Hall
City Centre
AA1 1AA

I am writing this letter to you to highlight the growing problems of vandalism within my home town. I am simply stunned and amazed that such degradation and vulgarity is not only allowed, but seems unchallenged by you and your colleagues.

On Tuesday night I drove into town to watch a concert at the opera house with my wife and two young children. Not only did it take two hours in horrendous traffic to reach my destination, but imagine my horror when my young children repeated the phrases spray painted on numerous walls during our journey.

I have contacted the local Police and expressed my concerns but they state in part that the matter is one for the council to attend to, but I have been promised that they will look into the matter further.

Is it not possible for you to fit CCTV cameras in the area or simply paint over the religious hatred which infects our town's walls and pavements? I am not only sick to death with facing newly built mosques in my area, but feel, as a law-abiding Christian man, my opinions no longer count.

I doubt I'll get any sort of response from you but I'll await your reply.

Regards

Mr A Smith

The Mayor of Your Town
Town Hall Chambers
Town Hall
AA1 1AA

Today's date

The Local Councillor
Town Hall
City Centre
AA1 1AA

Memo – Application for congestion charge

I have overlooked your proposal to introduce the congestion charge within the town centre and simply find it preposterous that you intend to tax constituents who enter and drive within the area highlighted on the map you supplied.

We, as a nation, today have the right to travel as we like without fear of further taxes being levied against us. It is our moral right to do as we please and as long as no persons within our constituency are physically harmed, then long may it remain that way.

I am therefore going to veto your application at the next council meeting but will seek the views and opinions of other council members before taking this matter any further.

May I also bring to your attention the up-coming deputy mayorship position and the vote which will be held next Thursday in the great hall! I would like to put forward the name of Mrs Jenkins as she has worked tirelessly as head of the committee for some years and I feel she will bring not only a wealth of experience but freshness to a somewhat stagnated post.

I do hope for and insist on your full support with this matter.

Will you also propose recommendations to target the increase of dog fouling within the town centre? I have received numerous complaints and want actionable ideas soonest.

The Mayor

WHAT TO DO NEXT

As with the first written exercise, the test now asks you to compose a written response to both parties, suggesting potential solutions to the problems highlighted. Remember to write the letter professionally and use correct punctuation.

> # WAIT!

As an author, my intention is to fill each page with useful information that makes you read on. However, to test you further, I now want you to close the book for a short time and on a scrap piece of paper formulate your response to this exercise. **Do *not*** refer back to both letters. I simply want to test you on how much – or little – information you have read and absorbed. You may be surprised either way.

Remember, on the day of the assessment you'll probably be suffering from nerves and stress. Practise the retention of information. I'll give you five minutes.

If you don't have paper to hand, then use the space provided below to either:

1. Write a response in letter form as you would on paper. *Or:*

2. As with the first exercise, jot down all the salient points from both letters that you can remember which you would use later in letter form.

And remember, no cheating.

> *I was that nervous, I read the letters at least three times, but the words went in one ear and straight out the other.* (Quote from a Constable)

PRACTICE SPACE

So how did you do?

HOW IT SHOULD BE DONE

Below is how I'd briefly respond to Mr Smith. My response to the Mayor would be similar.

The Local Councillor
Town Hall
City Centre
AA1 1AA

Today's date

Mr A Smith
3 Your Street
Your District
Your Town
Postcode

Dear Mr Smith

Thank you for your letter detailing your concerns about continuing problems of vandalism faced within our society. I am sorry you felt your letter would be ignored and wish to reassure you that my colleagues and I take all complaints very seriously.

I have read your letter and noted you have already contacted your local Police Constabulary with regard to the matter. I have therefore contacted Inspector Jones at the local station and have set up a meeting with him to formulate a more positive, proactive approach to this situation.

Neighbourhood Policing is of vast importance and not only will I, as your councillor, propose the installation of CCTV in the areas concerned, but will implement, wherever possible, a multi-agency approach consisting of high-visibility patrols from Community Officers, as well as utilising digital photography to record and document the increasing problem.

I will also endeavour to approach the Courts with the evidence collected and ask for those placed on community service orders to be tasked with painting over such graffiti.

I will also talk with youth services in the area to establish what contribution they can make to targeting the problem. We need, as a team, to endeavour to find ways in which to keep the young people of today busy with activities focused on fun and learning in an attempt to quell the problem.

Resolutions are also being sought with regard to congestion in the town centre and I now hope to put forward recommendations for a car-sharing policy which would seek to relieve certain parking charges or restrictions for those taking part.

Your feelings in this matter as a constituent are valuable to us. We seek to listen to all matters raised and endeavour as best as possible to act upon concerns raised. We must accept that today's society is a vast blend of cultures and beliefs and we feel this can only enrich our society further.

Please do not hesitate to contact us further should you need to do so.

Regards

Local Councillor

I know my example is short but I hope it gives you the idea of what is expected. The letter *must* be set out correctly, *must* use correct punctuation, *must* highlight and seek to achieve solutions to problems and *must* challenge any inappropriate content.

SUMMING UP

Whether good or not so, at least now you've an idea of what is expected and how adept you are at completing the task in hand. As with every other exercise on the Assessment day, it's all a matter of practice.

If you've taken your driving test, then remember how you performed on your first lesson and compare it to how you drive now. The more you do something, the better you become. The same principle applies with Police recruitment.

I now want to move on and in the next chapter we focus a little on the next section of the assessment centre process – the four interactive exercises.

6

The assessment centre – interactive exercises

The door opened and this red-haired man rushed towards me shouting at the top of his voice. I froze, mumbled something then cracked a joke. I don't think it went down that well. (Quote from a Community Support Officer)

You will now be involved in four role plays. Each one will be broken down into two phases.

PREPARING FOR THE EXERCISE

You will be handed documentation which will explain about the exercise you will undertake. You will have five minutes to read and digest what is required. For example:

You are a Customer Service advisor and will be faced with a member of the public dissatisfied with a product you produce. His child has nearly choked on a small part of the product and he blames you and the influx of non-skilled foreign workers entering the country.

WHAT YOU HAVE TO DO

You will then be guided to a room where a role actor will play the disgruntled customer. You will have five minutes to interact while being continually assessed on your performance.

This is the time to remember a few simple rules:

- *Listen* to the concerns and attempt to bring about logical *resolutions*.

- *Do not argue* with the role actor.

- *Do not raise your voice* – act calmly and sensibly throughout.

- *Adapt* your communication style accordingly.

- *Challenge* anything that breaches those core behavioural competencies.

In like a mouse, out like a lion.

The very first lesson I was taught when entering the Police Service was that of communication. *In like a mouse, out like a lion* simply means that, when faced with aggressiveness as you will be in these tests, do not start with your voice raised. If you do, it leaves you nowhere else to go. Start off calmly and gradually build up from mouse to lion status.

HOW DO I PUT THIS INTO PRACTICE?

Let's take the example of the disgruntled customer. You can almost guarantee when you walk through that door you'll be shouted at. Instead of attempting to match the role actor's voice, remain calm and speak clearly, explaining that in order for you to help, they are going to have to calm down and tell you exactly what their concerns are.

If they don't calm down, *try*, *try* and *try* again.

Listen to the concerns expressed to you and again, as in most tests, seek to achieve resolutions. Give the customer reason to believe in what you are saying.

Being forceful

Now that's not to say you can't be a little forceful from time to time. Assessors are looking for you to take control of the situation. If the role actor simply won't stop ranting and raving, then action needs to be taken. Do not shout at the top of your voice; simply raise yours in a calm authoritative tone.

Looking for challenges

The assessors are also looking for challenges. If the role actor suddenly comes out with a phrase such as:

> **... and that old fart next door is a waste of space ...**

then you will be expected to challenge this because it clearly comes under the heading of Respect for race and diversity. The role actor is testing whether you pick up on the matter of age discrimination, and secondly how you respond.

- If you simply nod and allow the rant to continue – grade **D**.

- If you challenge, explaining that language like that will not be tolerated and give reasons as to why – grade **A**.

HOW TO PRACTISE

Practice makes perfect I'm afraid. It may seem a little childlike or make you feel awkward but ask friends and family to help you. Let them make up scenarios and let you deal with them. It works, *honestly*!

I know an Officer who had a friend act for five days as an interviewer for a position the Officer was applying for. They both took it as a serious exercise and the Officer eventually passed his interview.

Practise!

7

The assessment centre – numerical reasoning test

WHAT TO EXPECT

For this part of the assessment process, you will be sitting with other candidates under exam conditions and asked to complete a set of numerical questions. These are not simple mathematical problems but are designed to test and analyse your problem-solving skills.

Now I can't take the test for you and have no way of knowing if, in a previous life, you used to be a mathematical genius or if you now come out in a rash every time you see a number, but the questions have to be answered.

HOW YOU SCORE

As with all the tests on the Assessment day, you will be graded from A to D. You are simply marked on a percentage. For example, if you score more than anybody else in the room on the test, you get an A. If your mind lets you down and you flunk the whole lot and all the candidates do better than you, you score D.

HOW TO PREPARE

All I can advise is that, prior to the tests, you get your mind active. Buy simple puzzle books from the local newsagents and do the odd crossword. Your mind is like a battery – make sure it is fully charged before the exam. It's a simple rule but one that works – practise, practise, practise.

AND REMEMBER – R.T.F.Q.

WHAT TO DO IN THE TEST

When seated in the test area, please pay attention to what you are being told. Nerves will sometimes cause you to miss individual snippets. Those little pieces of information missed might have helped during the exam. Try your best to remain focused.

During the test, the use of calculators or other such aids is forbidden. You may, however, use scrap paper to work out problems and those workings do not get marked.

My only advice for this stage is *balance*. As with my Sergeants exams, you need to slow your pace down so you have a clear understanding of each question but work quickly enough to answer all the questions.

HOW TO PRACTISE

In exercise 1 on page 70 I have supplied you with some questions of the types you are likely to face. Have a go and see how you perform.

EXERCISE 1

1. How much will five tins of peas cost at 14p per tin?

   A 60p   **B** 65p   **C** 70p   **D** 75p   **E** 80p

2. What is the average weekly wage of a team of five people whose wages are £56.00, £61.00, £66.00, £74.00, £83.00?

   A £66.00   **B** £68.00   **C** £70.00   **D** £79.00   **E** £86.00

3. A car is travelling at 72 miles per hour. How many miles will it have travelled in 45 minutes?

   A 48   **B** 50   **C** 52   **D** 54   **E** 58

4. Six magazines each contain 110 pages. How many pages are there in total?

   A 600   **B** 620   **C** 640   **D** 660   **E** 720

5. If my weekly paper bill is £4.50 and the delivery charge is an extra 35p per week, how much do I have to pay over six weeks?

   A £27.10   **B** £29.10   **C** £31.10   **D** £35.10   **E** £39.10

6. What is the average score per dart of a man who throws five darts and scores 14, 28, 51, 57 and 60?

   A 42   **B** 43   **C** 44   **D** 45   **E** 47

7. A Constable leaves the house at 07.00hrs and returns at 13.45hrs. How long have they been away from home?

   A 5 hrs 50 mins   **B** 5 hrs 75 mins   **C** 6 hrs 45 mins
   D 6 hrs 75 mins   **E** 7 hrs 25 mins

8. How many pieces of string 1.25m in length can be cut from a ball 100m long?

   A 80   **B** 85   **C** 90   **D** 125   **E** 140

9. If a car journey of 420 miles takes seven hours, what is the average speed of the car?

   A 55mph   **B** 60mph   **C** 65mph   **D** 70mph   **E** 75mph

10. If 70% of £450 has been spent, how much money remains?

   A £125   **B** £130   **C** £135   **D** £140   **E** £145

So those are the types of numerical questions you will be facing. I'm sure to some of you the puzzles above have come as quite a shock, especially without using a calculator. I'm also sure that some of you found them really easy. Whichever category you find yourself in, there's no harm in practising.

To see exactly how you did, check the answers given in Appendix 2 at the back of the book.

PRACTISING SOME MORE!

Like exercises elsewhere, try Exercise 2 below under exam-type conditions. Each question is similar to those in Exercise 1 and a space is left under each for you to write your answer.

Sit in a quiet room and have a stopwatch to hand. Do not use a calculator. These questions in part will be similar to the ones asked on the day; others will simply test your mathematical accuracy. Give yourself five minutes and try to concentrate throughout.

The answers are given in Appendix 3 at the end of the book.

TIP

Do not worry if you do not finish the paper on the actual test. It is more important that the answers you give are correct than a page full of mistakes. The test is also designed so that most won't finish anyway.

Oh my God, I've not done long division since school and even then I couldn't do it. How do you work out averages again?. (Quote from a Community Support Officer)

EXERCISE 2

1. **25 × 4 + 3**

    A 103   **B** 106   **C** 107   **D** 102   **E** 95

Answer _____

2. **48 divided by 6**

    A 6   **B** 10   **C** 8   **D** 7   **E** 12

Answer _____

3. **110 + 98 − 34**

    A 164   **B** 174   **C** 184   **D** 176   **E** 186

Answer _____

4. **115 − 34 + 19**

    A 99   **B** 100   **C** 108   **D** 107   **E** 120

Answer _____

5. **152 divided by 4**

    A 45   **B** 55   **C** 48   **D** 38   **E** 28

Answer _____

6. **What is the average of 9, 12, 13, 16 and 20?**

    A 10   **B** 11   **C** 12   **D** 13   **E** 14

Answer _____

7. **Divide the average of 15, 18 and 20 by 3**

 A 5.55 **B** 5.89 **C** 6.55 **D** 6.88 **E** 7

Answer _____

8. **What is the average of 34, 35, 36 and 40?**

 A 36.25 **B** 37.25 **C** 38.25 **D** 39.25 **E** 40

Answer _____

9. **Multiply the average of 6, 9, 4, 7 and 10 by 5**

 A 36 **B** 46 **C** 48 **D** 56 **E** 58

Answer _____

10. **What is the average of 7, 24, 86 and 45**

 A 39.5 **B** 40 **C** 40.5 **D** 41 **E** 41.5

Answer _____

11. **3 × 4 × 8 + 6**

 A 100 **B** 101 **C** 102 **D** 103 **E** 104

Answer _____

12. **6 × 6 + 8 × 4**

 A 58 **B** 68 **C** 78 **D** 87 **E** 97

Answer _____

13. **48 divided by 3 × 8**

 A 66 **B** 100 **C** 122 **D** 125.5 **E** 128

Answer _____

14. A man leaves home at 11.15hrs for a 45-minute car journey. He stops for 12 minutes for a coffee mid-way. What time does he arrive at his destination?

   A 12.00   **B** 12.12   **C** 23.12   **D** 00.00   **E** 00.12

Answer ....

15. A car travels at 40mph. How many miles would it cover in three and a half hours?

   A 140   **B** 145   **C** 150   **D** 155   **E** 160

Answer ....

16. If 14 tins of peas cost 18 pence each and you receive a discount of 50%, how much would 4 tins of peas cost?

   A 24   **B** 26   **C** 32   **D** 34   **E** 36

Answer ....

17. If a car travels for 2.5 hours at 14mph and an hour at half the speed, how many miles would it have travelled?

   A 29   **B** 34   **C** 38   **D** 42   **E** 45

Answer ....

18. If five pieces of rope equal 30 metres, what is the average length of each piece?

   A 9   **B** 10   **C** 8   **D** 7   **E** 6

Answer ....

19. A marathon takes 4 hours and 23 minutes to complete. It started at 09.45hrs. What time will it end?

A 13.00   **B** 13.08   **C** 14.00   **D** 14.08   **E** 02.08

Answer _____

20. If shopping is bought for £70 and 40 £1 coupons are used to pay as well as cash, how much cash would be spent with an added 25% off?

A £7   **B** £12.50   **C** £8.50   **D** £10   **E** £6.80

Answer _____

21. A school consists of 800 pupils. A quarter of the pupils are left-handed and a quarter of those have green eyes. How many pupils are left-handed with green eyes?

A 50   .   **B** 75   **C** 100   **D** 150   **E** 200

Answer _____

22. What is 9 – 15 + 18 divided by 3?

A 1   **B** 2   **C** 4   **D** 7   **E** 6

Answer _____

23. What is 189 divided by 36?

A 4   **B** 4.25   **C** 5   **D** 5.25   **E** 6

Answer _____

24. What is 45 × 15?

A 575   **B** 600   **C** 675   **D** 700   **E** 685

Answer _____

25. **What is the average of 19, 28, 132, 266, 12 and 89?**

   A 91 **B** 101 **C** 118 **D** 121 **E** 89

Answer _____

26. **A rally lasts for 36 hours and 12 minutes. The driver also takes three 12-minute breaks. If the rally started at 02.34hrs, what time will it have finished?**

   A 15.00 **B** 15.22 **C** 03.00 **D** 03.22 **E** 08.43

Answer _____

27. **5 + 115 + 213 + 678**

   A 1,011 **B** 1,000 **C** 998 **D** 760 **E** 1,232

Answer _____

28. **12,343 – 321 + 4,567 – 987**

   A 15,000 **B** 15,503 **C** 15,603 **D** 15,502 **E** 15,602

Answer _____

29. **What is 250 divided by 20 + 7.5?**

   A 10.25 **B** 15 **C** 16.5 **D** 18.75 **E** 20

Answer _____

30. **14 passengers board a train heading for London. Another 55 get on at Birmingham while 7 alight. At the next stop, of the 73 expected, only 69 take their seats. Jake leaves the train with 5 others prior to London because he is travel sick. How many passengers alight at London.**

   A 115 **B** 120 **C** 125 **D** 130 **E** 132

Answer _____

And Stop!

So how do you think you did? The answers are given in Appendix 3 at the back of the book. Please remember though, no matter how well you performed or how badly, practice does make perfect.

8

The assessment centre – verbal reasoning test

WHAT TO EXPECT

Again you will be under exam conditions and will be graded accordingly. This test will last 25 minutes and concentrate on how your mind absorbs all the information given to it, and how it reasons that information accordingly with a set of facts and statements.

For each question the facts will be set out something like this:

At the age of 18 years, Michael was flat broke so decided to burgle the local off-licence. At 23.00hrs he took a pair of bolt croppers and snapped the lock to the door. He subsequently stole £1,000 of cigarettes and two bottles of whisky. He was arrested the next day. The following information has been ascertained:

- Michael denied the offence on interview giving an alibi.

- Glynn had seen Michael on the day of the offence.

- The property stolen was recovered from a refuge bin.

- The shop owners do not wish to prosecute.

OK. So make sure you have understood the facts and taken in all the information. Next come the statements, for example:

(a) Michael is an alcoholic.

    A   B   C

From the instructions at the top of your question paper, you will know:

A   Corresponds to the statement being **true** given the situation described and the facts that are known.

B   Corresponds to the statement being **false** given the situation described and the facts that are known.

C   It is simply **impossible to say** whether the statement is true or false given the situation and the facts that are known.

So, in the example above, the correct answer would be C.

Let's try another:

(b) The offence was committed at 11.00hrs.

    A   B   C

Now: we must remember the following:

A   Corresponds to the statement being **true** given the situation described and the facts that are known.

B   Corresponds to the statement being **false** given the situation described and the facts that are known.

C It is simply **impossible to say** whether the statement is true or false given the situation and the facts that are known.

We can state correctly after reading the statement that the answer is B, false. The statement clearly says the offence was committed at 23.00hrs (eleven at night) and not 11.00hrs (eleven in the morning).

TIP

- *R.T.F.Q.* – Read the question more than once, slowly.

- *Do not jump to assumptions*. All the facts are written in front of you.

Again, I cannot take the tests for you but simply advise you on how best to go about each exercise. Remember you are being graded against all other candidates so do your very best, and remember – **DON'T PANIC**.

HOW TO PRACTISE

On the following pages I give you more examples like those we have looked at above. Try to practise and you'll soon get the knack.

Your mind has a tendency to jump to conclusions and using the common sense approach, give you answers that aren't actually on the page. Read what's in front of you, not what you think is. (Quote from a recruiter)

PRACTICE QUESTION 1

Twenty-five Officers attended work on Saturday morning to take part in Operation Gatecrasher. At 10.00hrs that day, five police vans containing all the fully briefed Officers attended at the target address where warrants were executed. Officers subsequently seized weapons, stolen property and drugs with a street value of £2,000. The following information has now been ascertained:

- Property stolen from a recent burglary was found in John's house.

- A cannabis factory was discovered.

- Four Officers were injured during the operation.

- Alex ran from the Police out of his back door and is now circulated as wanted.

(a) One weapon found was a 9mm pistol.

    A   B   C

(b) John is guilty of either handling stolen goods or burglary.

    A   B   C

(c) The three Officers injured were all assaulted.

    A   B   C

(d) Alex will be arrested.

    A   B   C

(e) Half a kilo of heroin belonged to John.

    A   B   C

PRACTICE QUESTION 2

Simon regularly drinks in a local public house that has recently been taken over by new staff. Since the takeover, unsavoury characters have begun to use the bar area and restaurant to sell large amounts of tobacco and spirits. Simon has seen many customers exchange money for these goods. He has subsequently reported his findings to Police. The following information has been ascertained:

- The Police have told Simon that they are aware of such activity.

- Simon recognises one of the sellers to be a local shoplifter.

- Simon has spent two years in prison for arson.

- A robbery occurred two weeks ago at a local off-licence.

(a) The items sold are from the robbery.

    A   B   C

(b) Members of the public have purchased items.

    A   B   C

(c) Simon's conviction was for arson with intent to endanger life.

    A   B   C

(d) The burglary at the off licence was captured on CCTV.

    A   B   C

(e) The Police may be planning an operation on the premises.

    A   B   C

PRACTICE QUESTION 3

While on routine patrol, PC Jones identifies a vehicle used in a local ram raid incident some hours before. He calls for further patrols and then approaches the vehicle which has been left unattended outside an address. Inside, PC Jones can see the vehicle has barrel damage and two crow bars are situated in the passenger foot well. The vehicle is subsequently removed for forensic examination. The following information is known:

- The ram raid was committed at 23.10hrs that night.

- Two crowbars were used to pry open the office door within.

- CCTV in the office was not recording at the time of the incident.

- The car is now parked outside of Jenny Smith's address.

(a) Jenny Smith is a local drug dealer.

    A   B   C

(b) Two males were captured on the CCTV within the office.

    A   B   C

(c) It is possible the crowbars in the vehicle are the ones used in the crime.

    A   B   C

(d) The incident took place at 11.10hrs.

    A   B   C

(e) The Police will search for fingerprints on the vehicle.

    A   B   C

PRACTICE QUESTION 4

Two males arrested for criminal damage are brought to the custody office for questioning. Both are put into cells and questioned separately regarding the allegation. Henry, the first to be interviewed, denies the allegation, stating he was sat at home with his girlfriend, Laura, at the time of the incident. Alan, the second to be interviewed, admits to smashing the window, stating it was Henry that passed him the rock. The following information is known:

- The incident took place within school grounds.

- Laura, a local student, was sitting her exams on the day in question.

- Mr Edwards, a teacher, saw two males running from the scene.

- Henry sports a full facial beard.

(a) Laura was with Henry when the crime was committed

    A   B   C

(b) The description provided by Mr Edwards describes a male with a beard.

    A   B   C

(c) The school was closed when the window was damaged.

    A   B   C

(d) Alan owes Henry money.

    A   B   C

(e) Alan threw the rock that smashed the window.

    A   B   C

PRACTICE QUESTION 5

On interview, Daniel, a prolific burglar, admits to breaking into five residential care homes over the last six months. He admits that his crimes were fuelled by an increasing drug habit and on most occasions he targeted petty cash and jewellery. He also admitted five counts of criminal damage and one count of assault. The following facts have been established:

- Six gold chains were found at Daniel's home when it was searched.

- Mary, a resident at a local care home, is Daniel's grandmother.

- Over the last six months, nine care homes have been burgled.

- Max, the local drug dealer, wants Daniel dead.

(a) Daniel is responsible for all nine burglaries.

    A   B   C

(b) It is possible the jewellery found is stolen property.

   A   B   C

(c) Daniel buys his drugs from Max.

   A   B   C

(d) Mary is Daniel's auntie.

   A   B   C

(e) Daniel's DNA led to his arrest.

   A   B   C

PRACTICE QUESTION 6

On Tuesday, 4 February, two new recruits started at the local police station. PC Thomas will tutor Katie and PC Reynolds will tutor David. Both PCs have been in the service for ten years and have been tutors for the last six. By the end of their first day, Katie had responded to 15 separate incidents and David seven. Two arrests were made which led to one charge and a court appearance. These facts are known:

- Katie used to work within the Youth Offending team.
- PC Reynolds will soon be transferring to another Force.
- The only arrests that day were for drink driving and public order.
- David has a minor conviction for being drunk and disorderly.

(a) Both student Officers work on the same shift pattern.

   A   B   C

(b) The combined service of PCs Reynolds and Thomas equates to 18 years.

   A   B   C

(c) Katie has a minor conviction for being drunk and disorderly.

    A   B   C

(d) A court appearance is likely for one of the arrests made.

    A   B   C

(e) PC Thomas has been a tutor for six years.

    A   B   C

PRACTICE QUESTION 7

A member of the public contacts Police via 999 at 02.45hrs. They report that six males are currently in a neighbouring scrap yard and are removing large amounts of lead from a workshop roof. The informant states that a vehicle is parked at the entrance gates to the compound with its engine running. There is a possibility that another male is in the driver's seat. The following information is also reported:

- Each person in the compound has a hood on with their faces covered.
- The yard belongs to ABC Engineering Ltd.
- A guard dog is barking in adjoining premises.
- The alarm has sounded and Police are already en route.

(a) There are a total of seven persons involved.

    A   B   C

(b) All persons involved are males.

    A   B   C

(c) The crime is being committed mid-afternoon.

    A   B   C

(d) Police are already aware of this incident.

    A   B   C

(e) The adjoining premises is named ABC Engineering Ltd.

    A   B   C

PRACTICE QUESTION 8

Lucy is walking along the high street at noon when she enters a clothing store. She carries a small rucksack and approaches the shoe section. She picks up a pair of trainers, asking the assistant for a pair in her size. While the assistant is distracted, Lucy quickly picks up another pair costing £120 and places them in her rucksack. As she attempts to leave the store an alarm sounds. The following facts are known:

- Lucy is a 26-year-old single mother.
- The security guard had apprehended one shoplifter today.
- The store's CCTV covers all sections of the store.
- The store manager prosecutes all persons found stealing from the store.

(a) Lucy is guilty of shoplifting.

    A   B   C

(b) The store manager apprehended Lucy.

    A   B   C

(c) The shoes are valued at £110.

    A   B   C

(d) The theft may be captured on CCTV.

   A   B   C

(e) Lucy has committed the offence of theft.

   A   B   C

To see exactly how you did, check the answers given in Appendix 4 at the back of the book.

SUMMING UP

The reasoning test sounds dead easy. When I practised, I got every single one right. You just don't expect your mind to suddenly seize up with the whole pressure of the day. Mine did and for a couple of minutes, I couldn't tell right from wrong. (Quote from a successful candidate)

So I hope now you're getting a fair idea of how the verbal reasoning test works and, more importantly, what assessors are looking for. Read what is in front of you and use it to get those questions right.

In the next chapter we move on to the final part of the day – the interview.

9

The assessment centre – the interview

WHAT TYPES OF INTERVIEW ARE THERE?

Before I talk about the interview stage in any more detail, I would like to bring to your attention a small fact. During the recruitment process you will undergo two interviews. The first, as discussed here, is included as part of the assessment day and comprises four questions, each with a time limit of five minutes per answer.

The second interview is more commonly known as a board interview and this is the very last stage you will complete before being offered employment with whichever Constabulary you applied for. This second interview takes place after successful completion of the physical and medical tests.

The second interview will be chaired by a member of the Human Resources department and include an Officer from your Constabulary. The Officer is usually of senior rank, but it varies from force to force.

I bring this fact to your attention for one purpose only. Even though both interviews are structured differently, you must act and behave in the same way for both. Both the assessment day and board interviews are marked using the same criteria, with very similar questions.

Therefore I urge you, should you reach the final stage of recruitment, to consult this chapter once again as it is designed to help pass both.

SO WHAT QUESTIONS WILL I BE ASKED?

If I knew the answer to this question, I'd probably know next week's lottery numbers as well! It's impossible to say. They are picked from a question bank of hundreds. All I can say is that they will be similar to those asked in the application form.

Below I've listed some of the possibilities. Please practise answering them but remember, on the day, they might be completely different.

SAMPLE QUESTIONS FOR PRACTISING

- Why do you want to join the Police Service?

- What skills or abilities do you think you possess that make you suitable for the role?

- How have you prepared for this interview?

- Explain when you have faced conflict and how you dealt with the situation.

- When have you had to make a choice in life that was important?

- Why do you want to join your particular Constabulary?

- Have you ever faced criticism? What happened and how did it make you feel?

- How do you relax after a stressful day at work?

- How do you handle stressful situations and how does it make you feel?

- When have you had to persevere with something?

- In the last six months, have you faced a particular problem? If so, how did you resolve it?

- What is your greatest achievement?

- What role in society do the Police have?

- Describe a time when you have acted as part of a team and explain how your role contributed to the team's success.

- How would you combat anti-social behaviour within a community?

- In the last six months, when have you been in contact with another person who has had very different beliefs, opinions or lifestyle to yourself?

- You are working with a colleague who makes an inappropriate remark about another female colleague. What would you do?

HOW TO STRUCTURE YOUR ANSWERS

As with completing your application form, you must use the same three principles when orally answering the questions put to you.

R.T.F.Q.

Now I know at this stage you're not exactly reading a question but the same principle applies. Listen to what you are being asked. Take in all aspects of the question and, before you answer, formulate your response in your head. There is nothing more uncomfortable than getting halfway through your answer and then stopping because your mind has gone blank. Know exactly what you are going to say before saying it.

Secondly, there is absolutely nothing wrong with asking the interviewer to repeat the question. You will not lose any marks because nerves got the better of you.

S.T.A.R.

You've understood the question and worked out an appropriate response in your head. Structure your response so you clearly demonstrate the S.T.A.R. principle. Explain the **situation**, then explain what **task** was set because of it, followed by your **actions** and the **result** of your actions as a conclusion.

Personalise

Again, as you did with the application form, personalise your answers. You are sat in front of the assessors for one reason: they believe you may be capable of doing the job applied for. If they didn't believe such a thing, you would have failed the application process long before. Now is your time to show them exactly how *good* you are.

Use the three principles in both the assessment day and board interview and if you can give relevant, pertinent answers to the questions, you stand more of a chance than most of progressing.

WORKING THROUGH AN EXAMPLE

Let's take the first sample question above as an example and answer it using the three tips I have given you.

Q. Why do you want to join the Police Service?

R.T.F.Q.

Firstly, formulate a plan for your answer. In the spaces below, write down five reasons why you want to join the Police Service.

(a) _____

(b) _____

(c) _____

(d) _____

(e) _____

My example would probably read something like:

(a) It has been a lifelong ambition to join the Police.

(b) I would like to work in a job where I can try to make a difference.

(c) I have a strong interest in criminal law.

(d) I would like to serve society and give something back.

(e) I like helping people.

Now I really cannot remember exactly what I said when asked this question some years ago but I'm sure the five points I have raised are similar to how I responded then.

S.T.A.R.

So now we have ideas as to how to answer the question, which we must explain using the S.T.A.R. principles.

Look at your very first point and write in the space below your answer to the question using S.T.A.R.

By now I hope that you can see how breaking down a question and examining each individual part helps you to give a more rounded, comprehensive answer.

Personalise

Let us now take my point, (It has been a lifelong ambition to join the Police), and using the S.T.A.R. principles, answer the question.

Q. Why do you want to join the Police?

A. Since childhood I have always harboured an ambition to join the Police Service. There were times whilst being at school that I attended career talks given by serving Police Officers who would explain as best they could the job they do and what a rewarding career it was to pursue.

So now I've demonstrated briefly the situation which led me to join.

Prior to reaching my 21st birthday, I knew that I still had my ambition to join so I tried to keep myself as physically fit as possible. Even though I was still too young to join, I began moulding my lifestyle to give me the best possible chance of success when the time came.

So my task was to become a Police Officer by moulding my life.

I began researching the role of a Police Officer using all available outlets open to me at that time to stand the best possible chance. I regularly visited libraries where I developed a basic understanding of criminal law and made efforts to speak with serving Officers at my local station who gave relevant and pertinent advice. When I then applied, I felt I had all the necessary tools to be successful in my application stage.

Those were my actions, gaining knowledge and experience

I was subsequently overjoyed when I heard the news I had passed the application stage which led me to where I am now.

This was the end result.

All this seems hard work I know, but setting your examples down on paper before even attempting to answer off the cuff allows you to develop a routine. If you can practise now, with the questions I have supplied, by the time you're sat in front of assessors, it should be second nature.

Now practise writing a full and comprehensive answer for the first sample question, using all points you raised, (a) to (e), on page 92.

SOME TIPS FOR PASSING BOTH INTERVIEWS

1. *Listen* to the question being asked. If you are unsure about any point – ASK.

2. Keep your answers *relevant* to the question asked. *Do not ramble*.

3. Structure your answers using the *S.T.A.R.* principles.

4. Speak *clearly* to the *face* of the interviewer. *Make eye contact*.

5. *Do not lie*. If you start making up stories, you'll sound idiotic.

6. I know you're nervous but *smile*.

7. *Use non-verbal communication*. Do not fold your arms or wave them frantically about. Interlock your fingers and rest them on you knees.

8. *Personalise*. This is the one true opportunity to impress the assessors. They want to know about YOU – **tell them**.

9. *No jokes* – this is not a stand up routine.

10. Structure your answers around the *core competencies*.

I was sat there with my knees knocking together and every time I tried to talk, I could hear a strange squeaking sound where my voice used to be. (Quote from a Police Constable)

10

The physical

Christ, that bleep test is a lot harder than I remember it to be!
(Quote from the author)

FOCUSING ON YOUR FITNESS

The role of an operational Police Officer demands a certain level of physical fitness. On regular occasions, you will find yourself either running after individuals or being involved in scuffles which require a certain amount of physical exertion. I would say that almost 80% of front-line Officers I currently serve with keep and maintain their fitness, either by visiting a gym regularly or simply going for the occasional run. There are some (and this certainly ***does not*** include me) that go for a run while on refreshments (a Police term for a lunch break).

I would also urge you that, should you be successful in your entire application and one day find yourself in a role within the Police that does not focus on fitness, to keep up your standards no matter what. I have found myself in one such role and for month after month feasted on nothing more than kebabs, burgers and other such crap. I smoke 20 a day and am quite partial to an alcoholic beverage. Put together, my fitness hit an all-time low and I'd hate to have seen what some of my internal organs look liked.

Training for the physical

When I first applied to join the Police, the physical was entirely different to what it is now. I was dedicated to the post I was applying for so made the conscious decision to train my little socks off. If you've gone through the hell of applying and passing all stages leading up to this one, do not fail now. Just imagine going through the whole process again. I know people who did.

I used to live five minutes from a local park which had a reservoir two miles in diameter. To this day I have no idea just how I did it, but every morning, come rain, wind or snow, I'd be there, 5.30 in the morning running twice around its shores.

I'd go to work and when I returned I'd spend about an hour on my little multi-gym in the back bedroom. I would lift heavy weights and buy body-building magazines to expand my knowledge on the different exercises and routines that would build maximum muscle. I followed this routine for about 12 months and by the time I first took my physical I breezed through, hardly breaking into a sweat.

Then and now

When I joined, the process and stages of recruitment were in a different order than they are now. You started with the application form, and once successful were invited to sit a numerical and English exam. Following these, some months down the line, an invite was sent to take part in a physical and only when passed would you endure the assessment day. Weeks after the assessment followed a board interview and only after passing that, would you be allowed to attend the medical.

It is my opinion – and I reiterate it is my opinion – that some aspects of the recruitment process for today's candidates are far easier to pass than back in my day, for example the physical. On the other hand, I would not like the prospect of facing today's assessment day.

Your personal fitness

No matter what I believe about the physical, it is not me that has to take it. I do not know each individual reading this book and do not know and cannot assess your current fitness level. For some of you, I'm sure that you may never have participated in any sort of exercise, no matter how many New Year's resolutions you've made. For others, you may not need to train any more than you do, but simply customise your current routine to ensure maximum benefit when the day arrives.

Whichever category you fall into, always remember there is plenty of time to adapt to the challenge ahead. Start slowly and allow your body to adapt to the excess of exercise. However, take heed – do not run before you can walk. You may strain or pull a muscle or injure yourself in some way, and sometimes the damage can be lasting.

If in doubt …

I am not a fitness expert by any stretch of the imagination so if you feel in any way dubious about starting any type of exercise routine, either anaerobic or cardiovascular or perhaps a mixture of the two, consult your doctor who may recommend certain dietary plans or exercise routines.

What's to come

On the following pages I will discuss in detail the physical and the medical and the standards you need to achieve in both. I may well recommend certain training techniques to help you achieve the standard expected. I once again reiterate that these are the routines which I followed so they may not be appropriate for other individuals.

I would first like to explain a little of what my physicals were like before we look at what is now expected of you.

PERSONAL EXPERIENCES

My first physical

My first physical was back in 1997. I had received a letter from the Police recruiters, requesting I attend the gym area of my Constabulary's training school to be assessed on my physical fitness. I was overjoyed and on the day packed my t-shirt, jogging pants and trainers and made my way with few nerves and a proud smile.

Upon my arrival, I introduced myself to some familiar faces that I had remembered from sitting my initial exams and waited for the assessors to arrive. When they did, the fun began.

The first stage of the process was to be weighed and measured so as to calculate my height/weight ratio and have my body fat tested. I was pleased to learn that at 5ft 10 and 11 stone, my body fat came in at 12%, which is not that bad at all.

We then took individual turns to test our grip strength. I was handed a small piece of equipment that my fingers wrapped around and, after starting the exercise, was told to grip the handle as hard as I could, three times in a row. My score was highlighted on the digital LED attached to the small piece of equipment. If you did not get the required score on all three tries, you were going home to have an early shower.

Next came the shuttle run (I will explain more about this a little later). I felt confident because of all the training I had done and this was to prove right. All candidates had to reach level 8.3. Some failed and were sent home. I managed 11.5.

I was then partnered up with another candidate and asked to perform as many press-ups in a one-minute time frame as possible. All candidates were asked to perform the press-up so that the chest touched the fist of the partner which was placed on the ground beneath. My score of 80 was not the best, but enabled me to progress further.

Again, those candidates who were still in the running were then asked to perform as many sit-ups and jumping jacks as possible. I cannot remember my final score but I passed and left that day with such high expectations of myself. Little did I know that I'd be back a few years down the line to do the whole process again!

Doing it again – with a difference

I had to wait a few years (three to be exact) before my next attempt at Police recruitment. Again, I passed all stages before me and was once again asked to attend for a physical.

In 2000 I attended the exact location of my first physical, still with a good level of personal fitness and a more intense passion to achieve my goal of attaining Police Constable status. I was still regularly training and felt I knew exactly what I needed to do. To my shock, the physical assessment had little resemblance to my first.

The grip strength which acted as the introductory factor in the first physical was no longer included in the syllabus. Instead, after the routine height/weight ratio check, it was straight into the shuttle run (more commonly known as the bleep test). The level which you had to achieve had been lowered so I once again passed with flying colours.

I do not know how they calculated the next section of the assessment, but I was then told that I would now be performing press-ups. The assessors had worked out an equation between my height and weight which gave an answer as to how many press-ups I needed to complete. Gone were the days of doing as many in one minute as possible. Now I had a number to reach. I was shocked, and nearly laughed when they informed me that my grand total would be 15. *Yes 15*!

Needless to say I passed and the 12 sit-ups to follow were almost a joke.

The final test for the day was to perform strength tests on a machine pulley that calculated how many kilograms you could push and pull. The equipment resembled a rowing machine found in most gyms, and had a bar type handle which could either be programmed to cause resistance when you pulled it or pushed it. I passed, only this time I didn't allow my emotions to get carried away.

Keeping up your fitness

I have now served many years in the Police Service and know the huge importance of physical fitness. Throughout your training and career, no matter how hard you find exercise, you need to keep it up for two specific reasons:

- your own personal safety;

- attendance at training days where physical exertion is a must.

Now it's about time we had a look at what you'll be doing on the day.

WHAT MAKES UP THE PHYSICAL ASSESSMENT?

1. Push 34kg and pull 35kg on a dynamic strength machine.

2. Four shuttle runs (bleep test) to level 5.4.

So there it is on a plate. You will be asked to take part in both sets of exercises with generous warm-ups beforehand. Do not take any of the exercises for granted. Even now, as you read this book you may be thinking:

Is that it?

Don't. Confidence is no bad thing but overconfidence can also hinder your progress. Prepare yourself physically and mentally and for the two or three hours the physical takes, give 100% effort and focus, because, if you pass this stage, you're almost there.

Anyway, let's talk about your physical in a little more detail. Let us start with number two on the list, the shuttle run, and work backwards.

WHAT IS A SHUTTLE RUN?

This test is designed for one purpose only, to test your endurance. You'll be asked to start at one end of the gymnasium behind a predetermined line shown to you by the assessor (it's usually coloured either red or yellow). When the test starts, you'll have to run to the other end of the gym, reaching another line. The length of the run is about 15 metres each way.

When it's time to start you will hear an audible 'bleep' and this indicates the test has begun. You must make your way to the other line at the opposite end of the gym, passing your foot over it. Your foot must be over that line before the next 'bleep' sounds.

When you place your foot over the line and the next 'bleep' sounds, you must run back to where you first started, making sure once again your foot crosses the predetermined spot before the next 'bleep' in the sequence.

You will find that at the very start you can pace yourself slowly. As with all shuttle runs, the 'bleep' sound will become a little quicker every phase. You will find that your nice leisurely jog at the start of the test, soon becomes a run, ending in a frantic sprint, depending on the level you've attained.

How are the levels measured?

Let's say, for example, you were required to reach level 5.4 as my Constabulary expects. Each level combines six runs. So, for example, if I were to run a total of six times up and down the gym (three one way and three the other) then that would constitute one level.

So we can now determine that to reach level 5.4, you will need to run up and down the gym a total of 34 times, with the bleep getting a little faster throughout.

EXAMPLE

6 × runs per level × 5 levels = 30 lengths + 4 = 34

You will be required to perform 4 × shuttle runs and expected to attain or go beyond the level each time.

What if my foot doesn't cross the line before the bleep?

Don't panic. You simply receive a warning so do your very best to catch up. However, remember – three warnings and you're out! Although this test assesses cardiovascular endurance it also tests your timing.

I have seen people who have been in top physical shape wither on this test, either because they start too quickly with the sole intention of getting that foot across, or simply unable to pace themselves with the bleep adequately enough and find themselves playing catch-up.

TIP

As you progress through each level, try to set off on the next phase with the opposite leg from which you did the last. If you don't, you'll soon find one of your calves burning in pain.

How can I practise at home?

You really have three options open to you.

1. Start jogging on frequent occasions. Go to your local park or simply run on the streets. Regular exercise of this standard will improve not only your cardio; it will firm the muscles in your legs and stomach. You can always introduce interval training to avoid boredom. Here is an example I used myself:

    (a) Begin your run at a nice easy pace, controlling your breathing as you run.

    (b) Choose a landmark up ahead of you, for example a lamp post or other item of street furniture.

    (c) Continue with your jog and when you get to the chosen landmark break into a sprint for 30 seconds or until you reach a second pre-determined landmark.

    (d) After passing the second landmark, slow once again into your regular jog, controlling your breathing throughout.

This exercise will improve your cardio vascular fitness no end. The other options are:

2. Become a member of your local gymnasium and enlist the help of fitness instructors to devise a specific training routine, for your body shape and current fitness level.

3. You can purchase the bleep test as a tape, CD, etc. Visit the Police training school for your area or any high-street sports/fitness shop, or go on-line. You will hear a bleeping sound which increases in speed at each level. The levels are split by an audible double bleep and notification from a narrator who, at the start of the exercise, will explain in detail how the exercise works. Practising in this way will not only build up your stamina, but will also give you a taste of how the test works and help you develop timing and pace.

No matter what example you follow, each is designed to help you through this part of the test. As with all the recruitment tests, from the application to the interview stages, the best advice I can give you is to practise.

Now let us talk a little about the strength tests.

WHAT ABOUT THE STRENGTH TESTS?

I would first like to draw your attention to a little fact. Every Constabulary's physical assessment differs and not all will include this next test. Those that do, however, may differ in either the exercises performed or the target score which you must achieve.

The shuttle run we talked of earlier is a universal tool, and not only do Police Services throughout the UK use it for measuring endurance, the Armed Forces and Fire Services also use it in their training schedules.

I can guarantee, though, that every Constabulary will include, as part of the physical, some means to measure your strength, either as in my previous attempts in which I was asked to perform exercises like press-ups, or by measuring your dynamic strength on a certain type of machine.

So it is of huge importance that, as for the shuttle run, you participate in exercises that will build your core strength. For those Constabularies that incorporate the dynamic strength machine, I will explain the basics behind the exercise.

A Police Officer not only needs the fitness level to be able to run after people, they also require a certain level of strength, because the sad fact of the matter is, you will be involved in fights, people will want to assault you and you will have to break up squabbles.

During my service, I have been assaulted and literally had fist fights with offenders. I have been grabbed and I have held onto those wishing to escape. You really do need the confidence in your ability to stand up to these types of occasions and display, not only strength of character, but sometimes bodily strength as well.

How it works

The dynamic strength machine measures upper body strength. You will be seated on the machine and it will be adjusted so you can grip the handles on both sides comfortably. The test will then be explained and warm-ups allowed.

It will be explained to you that, in the first exercise, you will push the bar away from you in a controlled manner as hard as you can. You will be allowed three warm-up attempts before performing five all-out pushes.

Your aim is to release as much explosive power as you can to achieve the required score. You must push and reach a power ratio of 34kg. Anything under is simply not good enough.

Next, the machine will be reprogrammed so that you no longer have to push the bar; you must pull it back towards you instead. Again, as with the push, you will be allowed three warm-up attempts before five all-out efforts.

Again, use your explosive strength and get that bar back as quickly and powerfully as possible. This time you must score the equivalent of 35kg per pull.

I also want to remind you, that unlike all other sections of the recruitment phase when you are graded against fellow candidates, the physical is a simple *pass or fail*.

How can I practise at home?

As with practising the shuttle run, you do have certain avenues open to you. They are:

1. Do as I did. Either use your body weight to perform such exercises as press-ups, squats, dips, etc., or invest a little money in a home gym, comprising free weights (dumb bells and a barbell) and a weight bench. The investment will be of use because you will still be able to use the equipment long after your success.

2. Join your local gym and use the weights room to build core strength and muscle mass. Your fitness instructor can advise you on the best exercises for your shape, age, sex, weight, etc.

In fact, any exercise that causes your muscles to work harder than usual will be of benefit, but please remember, if in any doubt, consult your doctor before participating.

WHAT IF I FAIL MY PHYSICAL?

All is not lost should you manage to fail on the first attempt. Most Constabularies now hold a 'three strikes and you're out' policy. To put it more simply, you are now given three separate attempts to pass the physical. Should you fail the first attempt, you will be invited back some weeks later to participate again in all the assessment activities.

I know of individuals who have failed first time around for whatever reason, but know of nobody who has taken three attempts. If you find yourself on the third attempt and feel you are struggling, maybe its time to ask yourself:

Am I really suited for this position?

So I'm hoping the advice I have given you about the physical has motivated you enough to begin an exercise routine or develop an existing training schedule to fit in these types of exercises. Now before you put the book down and sprint out of the door sporting the latest sweatband, sit back a little longer and read about the medical in the next chapter.

AN INSPIRATIONAL TALE ...

At the beginning of the year, while sitting at work, surfing the works computer, I happen to stumble across a job advertisement for a highly specialised post within my Constabulary. A little bored and peeved with my current position I applied, quickly filling in the application form on-line and sending it off without a second thought.

Imagine my utter surprise when, by the end of the month, I received notification that I had passed the application stage (paper sift) and had now been invited to take part in the physical aspect of recruitment for the post.

The date I had been given was some two weeks away so I first made general enquiries as to what the day entailed. Like initial recruitment, the tests were exactly the same but I had to reach level 9.1 on the bleep test. Thinking back to my amazing 11.5 run many years ago, my confidence was boosted and I relaxed a little about the day ahead. Even so, I made the sacrifice of giving up cigarettes for the two-week period and ate nothing but healthy, clean food.

My healthy living lasted approximately four hours and twenty minutes until I found my appetite satisfied from another KFC and celebrated this fact with a cigarette in my works car park. Needless to say, as the days passed and the physical grew nearer, I became increasingly apprehensive about my impending performance.

On the day, I found myself in a waiting area with 12 other fit-looking candidates. I had assessed each one's fitness by mere sight alone and found I was probably the weakest there. My imagination had started to fail me before my body had even time to warm up.

I remember examining one individual. He must have been six feet two, wearing a tight running vest that did nothing to hide hours of gym work underneath. He wore professional running pants finished off with expensive looking trainers. My mind was now running on overtime.

I'm going to look so stupid today. There's no way I can keep up with him. I'm out of breath just thinking about the run! (Quote from the author just before my run)

Imagine my horror as we lined up for the bleep test, to find this Officer stood right next to me. I looked at him, smiled, said hello and then looked at the line at the other end of the gymnasium some 15 metres away with total anticipation. Our instructions were given and I soon found myself progressing through the levels.

Level 9.1 was a lot further than I had ever remembered and by level 8, my breathing had become heavy, my legs felt like lead and the guy next to me hadn't even broken into sweat.

Suddenly, at about level 8.4 or so, the muscular runner stopped. I do not know exactly why (because I couldn't exactly stop to ask) but he held his leg and looked in some amount of pain. I also noticed that another candidate had begun to get warnings for not reaching the line in time and not crossing his foot all the way across.

My confidence began to rise and the last few lengths of the gymnasium were tortuous. When I hit level 9, my legs had seized and I could barely place one foot in front of the other. With teeth gritted I held my breath and forced one more length. Crossing the line I knew I had passed and that honestly came as a real surprise.

And the point ...

I guess I'm trying to make a couple of really valid points when it comes to your fitness and the taking of your physical. They are:

1. If I can still do it, anybody can.

2. Train for the physical using techniques designed to aid you in each exercise.

3. Do not leave any of your preparation until the last minute. I did and my God I suffered.

Needless to say, I passed the day and now find myself waiting for a final interview before being offered the position. By the time you read my book, I will have either achieved my goal or will still be working in the position I am today. One thing is for sure, I'll use and adapt the techniques I have mentioned on passing the interview stage when the time comes.

> *I run five days out of seven and spend two hours a night at the gym. I can't believe what just happened.* (Quote from the fit looking runner)

In the next chapter we move on to the final stage in the whole process, the medical.

11

The medical

Over the last weeks and months, you have been assessed on your competency for the role. Your mind and knowledge have been stretched and your body put through its paces. Before you get handed a warrant card and invested with power, the recruiters still want to check your suitability. I know of no other career that asks so much of potential candidates prior to employment.

IS THERE ANY ADVICE FOR THE MEDICAL?

There is not a great deal I can actually write about the medical as it really is quite straightforward, but if the prospect of attending a medical worries you in any way, I would recommend you speak with a doctor and ask them to perform a similar exam. This will firstly reassure you that your health really isn't all that bad, and secondly give an example of what a medical entails.

It is a sad fact of life and a more common occurrence among individuals today that we do not listen to our bodies enough. We ignore those little aches and pains or that lump until forced to attend for a check-up. It is also a fact that people who are one day healthy die the next due to undiagnosed diseases.

When I had my medical, I looked on it as if I was taking my car into the garage for a service. I know it can seem a little daunting, but let the medical practitioner do their work and put your mind, hopefully, at ease.

Now I'm not saying people don't fail this stage – they do. I know of some who have failed because they had never been diagnosed with colour-blindness or found to have a hearing defect or eyesight problems. The medical is rigorous but fair.

ON A SERIOUS NOTE

I would also like to remind those of you that have smoked a cannabis joint within the last few weeks that the Police Service will neither tolerate such behaviour, nor should they have to, and you will fail the medical outright. Cannabis takes six months to fully leave your body. Its particles stick to your hair and skin and the use of such substances can easily be detected through urine.

As with the physical tests described in Chapter 10, the medical also differs from Constabulary to Constabulary, although they all assess the same criteria. I can neither write nor give any helpful hints on the tests involved. Your health is simply that – *your* health.

All I can really do is explain a little about what I had to do many years back in an attempt to ease any fears you have about the day. The medical itself will usually take place at your Constabulary's training school, which should encompass a welfare department (which looks similar to a civilian clinic) and lasts for approximately two hours.

WHAT TO EXPECT IN THE MEDICAL

Eyesight test

This is quite straightforward really and I'm sure, like I have, you may have been tested before either at school or for the fitting of glasses. My test was exactly the same as taken by an optometrist. Whether yours will vary I do not know, but the same principle applies. Your Constabulary is making sure your eyesight is in the best shape possible for the role applied for.

Hearing test

I had to sit in a large cylindrical soundproofed booth and was handed a small buzzer. When the test began, I was asked to listen for a bleep and press the buzzer every time I heard one. The bleeps eventually became quieter and quieter until they finally disappeared. My results were monitored by the practitioner and my score recorded.

Lung capacity test

This is similar to a test taken to measure asthma! You take the apparatus in your hand and, when asked to do so, blow as hard as possible for as long as possible. The test measures how much air your lungs need to fully inflate.

Heart rate

You may have proved your worth in the physical but the assessors could not measure what amount of pressure your heart was under during the physical exercise. Your heart is the most important muscle in your body and not only needs to be trained accordingly, it also needs to be monitored as to how efficiently it performs under stress.

I was asked to perform stepping movements on a small box (exactly the same as step aerobics) for two minutes in time with a gradually increasing bleep. This test gradually causes your heart rate to quicken and can be monitored throughout.

At the end of the test, your heart is also tested on how quickly it can recover from such intense activity.

Provide a urine sample

You will be handed a small plastic container and asked to provide urine. The sample is then taken into an office for testing. The only small hint I can give you here is drink a couple of cold beverages before you attend the medical, so when the time comes, you will be ready to pass water. You will not be allowed to leave the medical until a sample has been provided and tested. I remember one individual I took my medical with sitting in the reception area with his little empty cup for two hours until he managed to go.

The practitioner simply dips a special strip into your urine and notes the subsequent colour change. Each colour represents different things and can highlight both medical problems such as water infections or sexually trans-mitted diseases, and also indicates any use of illegal substances.

The gentleman's test

For all males preparing for the medical, its now time to make sure you've a clean pair of underwear on. You will be asked to lower your trousers and undergarments and, while a hand is placed underneath your testicles, asked to cough. I don't think I need to elaborate any further.

SO THAT'S IT …

So that's the medical, or at least the one I took some years ago. I'm quite sure it will have changed but the principles will remain exactly the same. You are being tested on your medical suitability for the post. You will be notified on the day of taking the test whether you have passed or failed. If you do fail, however, do not get disheartened. The practitioner will explain the exact reasons for failing and may have highlighted a medical problem that you were completely unaware of. Trust me, it's better to know.

If you get the go ahead and pass, you are as ready as you can be for that all-important board interview. Go back over the interview guidance I gave you in Chapter 4 – and good luck!

12

Conclusion

Whether you're already participating in the recruitment process or it's simply an ambition which you harbour and may act upon in the future, use this book as a tool to help you. In my time there was little information out there to assist me and I went into the recruitment process completely blind. Today, I urge you to prepare fully and research the role you are applying for.

IS IT WORTH IT?

The role I undertake allows me to see and do things that 90% of people could never imagine. There really is no other job out there like it. I routinely find myself on any given day attending such incidents as robberies, missing people and sudden deaths to the more obscure and abstract. I remember one such job, attending a flat simply because the occupant had reported to Police that she had an infestation of mice.

I know the recruitment process is a long and arduous one but the rewards far outweigh the initial efforts put in. If you really want to do this job, then go for it with all your might. You will find yourself working funny shifts with unsociable days off when all your friends are working, but it's worth the little extra hassle.

CARRY ON TRAINING!

Your training never really ends and continues throughout your time as a Police Officer. No matter what rank you achieve or position you hold, you learn and adapt on a day-to-day basis. I have gained skills and abilities that I never thought I had in me.

I wish you the very best of luck during recruitment and hope you achieve all you desire.

ONE LAST POINT ...

Before I end, I would like to give you one final hint, one which above all others I feel is most important:

> **If you find yourself working with a handsome young man with a goatee beard with slight flecks of grey in an immaculate head of hair, then I take coffee with two sugars and am always partial to a chocolate biscuit.**

Good luck again!

Kenneth

Appendix 1

Recruitment office contact details

FORCE	ADDRESS (For the attention of the Recruiting Department	TELEPHONE CONTACTS
Avon and Somerset Constabulary	PO Box 37, Valley Road, Portishead, Bristol, BS20 8QJ	01275 816142 / 6153 / 6360
Bedfordshire Police	Woburn Road, Kempston, Bedford, MK43 9AX	01234 842398
British Transport Police	PO Box 260, 15 Tavistock Place, London, WC1H 9SY	020 7388/9121
Cambridgeshire Constabulary	Hinchingbrooke Park, Huntingdon, PE29 6NP	01480 422734 / 422797
Cheshire Constabulary	Castle Esplanade, Chester, CH1 2PP	01244 614114
City of London Police	PO Box 36451, 182 Bishopsgate, London, EC2M 4WN	020 7601 2211 / 2252
Cleveland Police	PO Box 70, Ladgate Lane, Middlesbrough, TS8 9EH	01642 301459 / 301374
Cumbria Constabulary	Carleton Hall, Penrith, Cumbria, CA10 2AU	01768 217095
Derbyshire Constabulary	Butterly Hall, Ripley, Derbyshire, DE5 3RS	01773 572104
Devon and Cornwall Constabulary	Middlemoor, Exeter, EX2 7HQ	01392 452500

Dorset Police	Winfrith, Dorchester, Dorset, DT2 8DZ	01305 223794
Durham Constabulary	Aykley Heads, Durham, DH1 5TT	0191 375 2125 / 2369
Dyfed Powys Police	PO Box 99, Llangunnor, Carmarthen, SA31 2PF	01267 226441 / 226288
Essex Police	PO Box 2, Springfield, Chelmsford, Essex, CM2 6DA	01245 452277
Gloucestershire Constabulary	Holland House, Lansdown Road, Cheltenham, Gloucestershire, GL51 6QH	01242 276317 / 276684
Greater Manchester Police	PO Box 22 (S. West PDO), Chester House, Boyer Street, Manchester. M16 0RE	01618 562333
Gwent Police	Croesyceiliog, Cwmbran, Torfaen, NP44 2XJ	01495 745409
Hampshire Constabulary	Hamble Lane, Hamble, Southampton, SO31 4TS	0800 028 0222
Hertfordshire Constabulary	Stanborough Road, Welwyn Garden City, Hertfordshire, AL8 6XF	0800 358 3990
Humberside Police	Priory Road, Kingston upon Hull, HU5 5SF	01482 808051 / 808002
Kent Police	Kent Police College, Coverdale Avenue, Maidstone, Kent, ME15 9DW	01622 653394 / 653043
Lancashire Constabulary	PO Box 77, Hutton, Nr Preston, Lancashire, PR4 5SB	01772 410429
Leicestershire Constabulary	St John's, Enderby, Leicester, LE19 2BX	01 16 222 2222 ext. 2657
Lincolnshire Police	PO Box 999, Lincoln, LN57PH	01522 558235
Merseyside Police	PO Box 59, Liverpool, L69 1JD	0151 777 8253
Metropolitan Police	Simpson House, Peel Centre, Aerodrome Road, London, NW9 5JE	020 8358 0432
Metropolitan Police	Recruitment Hotline	08457272212
Norfolk Constabulary	Falconers Chase, Wymondham, Norfolk, NR18 0WW	01953 423823

Northamptonshire Police	Wootton Hall, Northampton, NN4 0JQ	01604 888033
Northumbria Police	Ponteland, Newcastle Upon Tyne, NE20 0BL	01661 868816
North Wales Police	Glan-y-don, Colwyn Bay, LL29 8AW	01492 510019
North Yorkshire Police	Newby Wiske Hall, Northallerton, North Yorkshire, DL7 9HA	01609 789079 / 789075
Nottinghamshire Police	Sherwood Lodge, Arnold, Nottingham, NG5 8PP	0115 967 0999 ext. 2425 / 6
South Wales Police	Cowbridge Road, Bridgend, CF31 3SU	01656 869225
South Yorkshire Police	Snig Hill, Sheffield, S3 8LY	01142 821234
Staffordshire Police	Cannock Road, Stafford, ST17 OQG	01785 235353
Suffolk Constabulary	Martlesham Heath, Ipswich, IP5 3QS	01473 613720
Surrey Police	Mount Browne, Sandy Lane, Guildford, Surrey, GU3 1HG	01483 482600
Sussex Police	Mailing House, Lewes, Sussex, BN7 2DZ	01273 404151
Thames Valley Police	Oxford Road, Kidlington, Oxon, OX5 2NX	01865 846816
Warwickshire Constabulary	PO Box 4, Leek Wootton, Warwick, CV35 7QB	01926 415052
West Mercia Constabulary	Hindlip Hall, Hindlip, PO Box 55, Worcester, WR3 8SP	01905 455051
West Midlands Police	PO Box 52, Lloyd House, Colmore Circus, Queensway, Birmingham, B4 6NQ	0121 626 5824 / 265 7007
West Yorkshire Police	PO Box 9, Wakefield, West Yorkshire, WF1 3QP	01924 292069 / 292164
Wiltshire Constabulary	London Road, Devizes, Wiltshire SN10 2DN	01380 799341

Appendix 2

Answers to numerical reasoning exercise 1

1. **C** 70   6. **A** 42

2. **B** 68   7. **C** 6 hrs 45 mins

3. **D** 54   8. **A** 80

4. **D** 660   9. **B** 60

5. **B** 29.10   10. **C** £135

Appendix 3

Answers to numerical reasoning exercise 2

1 **A** 103	16 **E** 36
2 **C** 8	17 **D** 42
3 **B** 174	18 **E** 6
4 **B** 100	19 **D** 14.08
5 **D** 38	20 **B** £12.50
6 **E** 14	21 **A** 50
7 **B** 5.89	22 **C** 4
8 **A** 36.25	23 **D** 5.25
9 **A** 36	24 **C** 675
10 **C** 40.5	25 **A** 91
11 **C** 102	26 **B** 15.22
12 **B** 68	27 **A** 1,011

13 **E** 128

14 **B** 12.12

15 **A** 140

28 **E** 15,602

29 **E** 20

30 **C** 125

Appendix 4

Answers to Practice questions

PRACTICE QUESTION 1 ANSWERS

(a) The answer is **C**. It is impossible to say with the facts established, what weapons were found.

(b) The answer is **A**. Since stolen property was found within John's house, he will be arrested and questioned with regard to the offences mentioned.

(c) The answer is **B**. Four Officers were injured, not three.

(d) The answer is **A**. Alex will be arrested as the statement and facts clearly state that he has been circulated as wanted.

(e) The answer is **C**. Although the statement mentions drugs, it does not state what specific drugs were seized apart from cannabis.

PRACTICE QUESTION 2 - ANSWERS

(a) The answer is **C**. It is impossible to say whether the items are from the robbery.

(b) The answer is **A**. The statement clearly states customers have exchanged monies for goods.

(c) The answer is **B**. Simon was convicted for arson and not the more serious office of endangering life.

(d) The answer is **B**. The off-licence was subject to a robbery, not a burglary.

(e) The answer is **A**. Within the facts it is established that the Police are aware of activities in the public house.

PRACTICE QUESTION 3 – ANSWERS

(a) The answer is **C**. It is impossible to say whether or not Smith is a drug dealer.

(b) The answer is **B**. There is no CCTV as the camera in the office is not working.

(c) The answer is **A**. It is highly likely the crowbars found were those used in the crime.

(d) The answer is **B**. The crime was committed at 23.10hrs at night, not 11.10hrs in the morning.

(e) The answer is **A**. The car will be taken for forensic examination.

PRACTICE QUESTION 4 – ANSWERS

(a) The answer is **B**. Laura was sitting exams at the time and not with Henry.

(b) The answer is **C**. With the facts known, it is impossible to say what description was given.

(c) The answer is **B**. The school was open because Laura was taking exams and the teacher was present at the time.

(d) The answer is **C**. With the facts established, there is no mention of Alan owing Henry money.

(e) The answer is **A**. Alan threw the rock that smashed the window.

PRACTICE QUESTION 5 - ANSWERS

(a) The answer is **C**. It is impossible to say with the facts established whether Daniel committed all nine burglaries.

(b) The answer is **A**. The jewellery may be stolen as it is mentioned that Daniel targets such property.

(c) The answer is **C**. There is no evidence to suggest Daniel buys from Max so it is impossible to say.

(d) The answer is **B**. Mary is Daniel's grandmother, not auntie.

(e) The answer is **C**. There is no mention of DNA in all the facts before us.

PRACTICE QUESTION 6 – ANSWERS

(a) The answer is **C**. There is no mention of shift patterns in the facts so it is impossible to say.

(b) The answer is **B**. The combined service of both Officers is 20 years, and not 18.

(c) The answer is **B**. David has the minor conviction, not Katie.

(d) The answer is **A**. As a charge has been brought through one of the arrests, a court case would naturally follow.

(e) The answer is **A**. PC Thomas has tutored for six years as mentioned in the facts given to us.

PRACTICE QUESTION 7 – ANSWERS

(a) The answer is **A**. The facts tell us that six are in the yard and one in the vehicle, equating to seven in total.

(b) The answer is **A**. The facts tell us that the initial report states that all are male.

(c) The answer is **B**. The offence was committed at 02.45hrs in the morning, not the afternoon.

(d) The answer is **A**. The facts tell us that Police are already en route.

(e) The answer is **B**. Within the facts given, there is no name for the adjoining premises.

PRACTICE QUESTION 8 – ANSWERS

(a) The answer is **C**. We cannot ascertain from the information supplied, whether Lucy is guilty of shoplifting.

(b) The answer is **C**. There is no evidence to suggest that Lucy was apprehended.

(c) The answer is **B**. The shoes were £120, not £110.

(d) The answer is **A**. The incident might be captured on CCTV as it covers all the shop.

(e) The answer is **C**. As with the first question, we do not have enough information to make that decision.

Index